THE UNITED STATES CAVALRY
1865 - 1890
Patrolling the Frontier

ANDREA PRESS

Editorial Manager:
Javier Huerta

Author:
A. Mayoralas

Translation:
Sally-Ann Hopwood

Corrections:
Charles P. Davis

Illustrations:
José Ignacio Redondo

Published by:
ANDREA PRESS
c/ Talleres, 21 - Pol. Ind de Alpedrete
28430 Alpedrete (Madrid)
Tel.: 918 57 00 08 - Fax: 918 57 00 48
www.andrea-miniatures.com
andrea@andrea-miniatures.com

Photograph sources:
Corbis: 6, 7, 8, 9, 11b, 20, 21, 26, 31, 34, 35, 40, 41, 42, 44, 45, 48, 49,

Layout:
Andrea Press

Printed by:
Gráficas Europa

ISBN: 84-96527-87-5
Depósito Legal: S.1.535-2006

SUMMARY

The role of the U.S. Cavalry during the Indian Wars has been enormously embellished in popular culture. Taking part in the history of the Far West, it became a legend long before the appearance of the great American cinema productions. Hollywood has enormously increased the celebrity of those successes, creating a unique celluloid genre: The Western. The 7th Cavalry, led by General George Custer, Sioux, Comanche and Apache and battles such as Little Bighorn have fed the imagination of many generations and form part of universal mythology.

In truth, legend dilutes and blurs history while, at the same time, perpetuating it. Today, the Western appears to have almost deserted our cinema screens and, in the wake of new generations, the 'blue soldiers', guns and Indians have disappeared. This book provides a reliable approximation of how these military units were, in terms of their organisation strategy, uniforms, daily life, etc., as well as their battles in savage and hostile territories, confronted by able and terrible warlike peoples: The 'redskins'. It focuses on the height and the end of the Indian Wars, the period between 1865 and 1890.

The Indian Wars in the Middle of the 19th Century

Conflict with the Indian peoples of North America already began during the first years of colonisation of the territory. Subjugation had been completed by the close of the first half of the 19th Century. By then, the overwhelming force of the white man force had destroyed or displaced numerous tribes westwards. Colonisation reached a natural boundary west of the Mississippi River: Indian Territory. These vast stretches of land were still dominated by the natives and their nomadic way of life.

Towards the middle of the century, several decisive events took place in the history of the United States that would mark the beginning of a new era. The victory over Mexico in 1848 provided new and extensive territories to colonise. Meanwhile, the discovery of gold at Sutter's Creek in 1849 unleashed the so-called 'Gold Rush'. These events combined resulted in the fact that, step by step, an ever-increasing number of colonists migrated and settled in Indian Territory.

During the American Civil War (1861-1865), attention was diverted to this decisive and fratricidal conflict and the regular army units marched to fight important battles in the east. During this period, Indian incursions became more frequent, becoming almost daily occurrences, and local militia volunteers filled the void left by the regular army units. The confrontations were very savage, and the situation entered into a vicious cycle of violence. After the defeat of the (Confederates) southern states in 1866, migration became unstoppable and the government intervened directly to deal with the problem. All the treaties previously signed to respect the Indian peoples' territories were repeatedly broken in favour of the white man's interests. Conflict was inevitable.

Pioneers from the Indian lands who had returned to the eastern shores of the Mississippi spread rumours of riches and opportunities. These nourished the hopes of millions of poor colonists and adventurers in search of a better life. The exploitation and occupation was also promoted by proclamations such as Manifest Destiny, the moral justification for the expansion towards the Far West, and legislation such as the Homestead Act, a ruling that conceded 65 hectares of land to inhabitants settling for more than five years provided the necessary legal backup.

PATROLLING THE FRONTIER

The Cavalry Marches West

Once the Civil War was over, the Indians represented a small-scale problem for the governors and military men of the already great American nation. A wave of pacifism overtook the country and the President at the time, Andrew Johnson, decreased the size of the regular army. However, the Indian problem kept the frontier closed burning it became necessary to send in reinforcements. The cavalry was the most efficient weapon against the Indians and in spite of the fact that mounted units were expensive, four new regular cavalry regiments were created to reinforce the six existing ones. These ten cavalry regiments were positioned along the Great Plains, patrolling the vast territory and protecting the white man's interests.

The Indian Adversary

In 1865, it is estimated that 270,000 Indians lived in the territories along the western shores of the Mississippi River, which extended from the arid lands of New Mexico, Arizona and Texas to the green prairies of Montana. The redskins were not a united people, but rather disparate Indian nations following with different cultures. Each nation was divided into tribes and then into villages, small groups with a nomadic or semi-nomadic lifestyle; they were independent and took their own decisions.

The most important Indian nation was the Dakota generally known as the Sioux, a name encompassing tribes such as Brulee, Oglala, Hunkpapa, Sans Arc, Minneconju and a few smaller tribes. Other significant tribes included the Nez Percé, Crow, Cheyenne, Comanche, Arapahoe and Apache. They did not all live in peaceful coexistence; some were mortal enemies, while others upheld traditional alliances. In daily life, at times villages belonging to the same tribe would join forces to form warring parties or to celebrate certain religious rites. More commonly, however, villages were unrelated and wandered independently across the vast territories. Finding a camp of several thousand Indians became the most important military goal...

Wagon trains crossing the prairies along the crags of the Oregon Trail, the well-travelled access route to the land 'promised to the white man'.

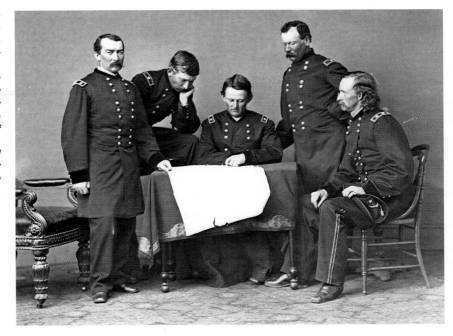

The internment policy of placing Indians on reservations that the U.S. government attempted to impose was not usually carried out in a humane or peaceful manner. The Indian Wars were directed by a military leadership that found it hard to come to terms with the new ways of war as waged by the Indians. The photo shows some of the leaders of these confrontations. From left to right, Generals Phil Sheridan, George Forsyth, Wesley Merrit, George Crook and George Armstrong Custer.

Patrolling the Frontier

Exercising control over such a complex number of Indian tribes and villages, dispersed throughout such a gigantic territory was practically impossible. When trying to reach a peace agreement, there was no one leader or group of leaders able to represent all the tribes and, even less so, to impose any agreement on them. Hence, during the Indian Wars, great battles were not a common occurrence, but rather the wars were characterised by hundreds of small, sporadic confrontations. This, then, was the reason why, once the Civil War was over, it took 25 years to subjugate the Native Americans.

The cavalry units were divided into garrisons, called frontier posts or forts, situated strategically along the frontier. Their mission was to guarantee the passage of the settlers and to protect farmers, miners, and railroad and telegraph installations and operators and any other interests of the white man. The most important actions usually took place during search and destroy campaigns against Indian settlements. It was these where the cavalry represented the most significant weapon in the persecution and eventual annihilation of the enemy.

All the army units and their respective forts formed part of a logistic and administrative organisation controlled from Washington D.C. that divided the country's territory into regions called Divisions, in turn broken down into Departments. The Pacific and Missouri Departments were primarily in charge of the Indian Wars.

'Visit to Another Tribe'
Painting by Edgar Samuel Paxon
As well as the usual problems and risks involved with any long, arduous journey, the settlers were always aware of the latent danger of the Indians, though not always in a warlike manner. The army, having to patrol vast expanses of land with scarce resources, was often not on hand to offer the required protection.

THE CAVALRY SOLDIER

Enlistment

Being in the cavalry was a hard career. It was full of risk, poorly paid and with very little social recognition. In the years following the Civil War, it was always possible to find war veterans without a second profession, poor immigrants, vagrants, drunks and men who 'needed to live above the law'. The army recruiters asked no questions and the doctors considered that if a recruit could walk he would do. This diversity of characters had little opportunity to become integrated in society and readily accepted an adventurous life in the open air, full of hardship for the meagre pay of just $13 a month. Let it not be said that they were all the dregs of society, some enlisted for romantic ideals, preferring adventure to the more boring life in the towns. Others were simply following a military profession and had either not been admitted or failed to graduate from West Point. Another important contingent, and with a colourful diversity were the immigrants that arrived in waves from Europe. Those from Ireland and Germany were the most numerous groups, with smaller groups from Britain, France and Italy. Indeed, the 7th Cavalry could have passed for a unit of the French Foreign Legion: In 1879, of its 793 troopers, 320 had not been born in the United States and were from 16 different nationalities. This situation was not exceptional. Many of the new recruits were 'fresh off the boat from Europe', spoke poor, or non-existent English and could neither read nor write. The diversity of origins also generated clans: The Irish were generally the least accepted, due to their lack of practical skills and their adherence to the Roman Catholic religion (this also applied to the Italians) in a country where the dominant religion was Protestant. The Germans were better received, as they generally had occupations useful in the Far West where everything was lacking.

'My Bunkie,' painting by the author Charles Shreyvogel. Recruitment propaganda offered an attractive life of adventure in the countryside and a possibility for inclusion into society for the least favoured social classes.

The level of skill taught in the recruitment centre was very low and it was not until 1880 that the new cavalry trooper left for his unit with even the minimum ability required for confronting the dangers that awaited him on the frontier. In this photo, a company of the black troopers, known as Buffalo Soldiers, is represented.

Enlistment in the cavalry also represented an opportunity for the black man. Some were veterans of units that had fought in the Civil War; others were freed slaves and cimarrones (1) in search of the security provided by the army's anonymity. No less than two cavalry units, the 9th and 10th, were made up of coloured troopers.

The average age for enlistment was 23 years old. However, at archaeological digs at a number of the battlefields, such as Little Bighorn, forensics have shown that some of the bones found belonged to men younger than 18.

Jefferson Barracks

All the cavalry volunteers began their military life at Jefferson Barracks in Missouri where, after routine physical training and the swearing-in ceremony, they signed an enlistment for five years, which was later decreased to three. Jefferson Barracks was not a training centre; no horse-riding techniques, weapons training, practising of military manoeuvres or the teaching of any tactic took place here. Once the recruits had been issued with their basic uniforms, they carried out routine, daily barrack tasks and learnt the basic ideals of the celibate and disciplined life. The maximum period of stay was four weeks, though this was often reduced to just a few days before sending the new troopers to their designated units.

The pitiful preparation with which the men left Missouri led to many complaints from the commanders and, from 1880, a program of four months military exercises was initiated, consisting of riding skills, learning the use of weapons, manoeuvres and a better knowledge of the military doctrine.

The Officers

The majority of the cavalry officers were graduates of West Point and were Civil War veterans. During the internecine struggle, many of them had attained much higher provisional ranks, even commanding divisions or brigades, due to the huge number of volunteer regiments created in order to win the war. Once the war was over, they became frustrated commanding a company or battalion with the corresponding lesser status and lower pay. The low wages and slow promotion did nothing to raise morale; in 1870 a second lieutenant earned just $115 a month while a colonel earned $300.

Even the long experience gained by these officers fighting the Confederate Army was insufficient to defeat their skilful, ferocious Indian warrior adversaries although, paradoxically, they were usually arrogant and vastly underestimated the worthiness of the Indian. The veteran nature of some officers also caused them to openly show disrespect to their superiors, many of who had occupied administrative positions during the war and had no direct combat experience. This led to numerous factions of veterans and disloyal captains and lieutenants.

(1) Escaped slaves taking refuge in the mountains and other hard to access places.

LIFE ON THE PLAINS

A Day on the Plains

Life at the frontier was extremely tedious: The monotonous noise of pick, shovel and wheelbarrow that extended day after day throughout the construction or improvements to the deficient forts and other frontier posts. Barrack tasks, such as the tedious guards duties, cleaning the privies and stables, serving in the hospital or kitchen, caring for the horses or cutting firewood, did nothing to help raise the troop's moral.

Occasionally, it was necessary to abandon the fort and carry arms. The most usual mission was to go in search of water or other provisions. Others were destined to set out on routine patrol, escort wagon trains and hunt down hostile Indian war parties. Even on these last occasions, contact with the Redskins was very rare, as the Indians tended to avoid direct confrontation although careful precautions had to be taken to avoid ambushes.

The truly adventurous lifestyle was experienced when on campaign. Large distances were travelled across unknown lands and never-ending plains. At night, when the weather was good, uninterrupted sleep was possible and during inclement weather, refuges were sought and the famous conical 'Sibley' tents were erected.

Training

The lack of economic resources, due to the penny pinching of the government, meant that the necessary firing exercises and weapons training, tactics and manoeuvres and horse riding were inadequate. The lack of ammunition meant that, for many troopers, a fight with Indians was their first combat experience without knowing how to adjust the sights of their carbine. From 1872 onwards, an official minimum of 40 cartridges was placed at the disposal of each trooper for firing practice although, in reality, the scarcity of ammunition in many garrisons was such that the allowance could not be fulfilled. Only units with renowned leaders, such as Custer's 7th Regiment and Mackenzie's 4th were able to instruct their soldiers in the use of arms, even managing to form a company of elite marksmen.

The Poor Diet

Food was both bad and scarce and Civil War supplies continued to be supplied for many years after the cessation of the conflict. These usually included salt pork, some beef, coffee (un-roasted and un-ground) and some biscuits, so-called 'hardtack', that were hard enough to break a tooth and required softening in liquid. These were used to make a type of highly nutritious broth by mixing them with fat and bacon. Depending on the distance from the fort and level of corruption of the quartermasters, other food such as barrels of potatoes, apples, onions, eggs and butter could also reach the soldiers. However, shortages were usually such that the troopers were forced to supplement their diet through pur-

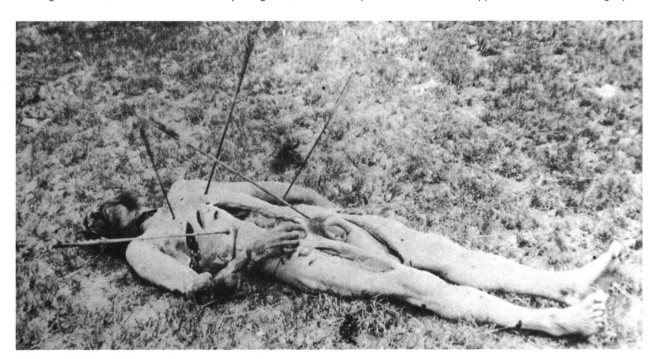

A gruesome act could take place suddenly, with an unexpected aftermath. The photo shows the body of Sergeant Frederick Wyllyams, Company G, 7th Cavalry, exactly as his comrades near Pond Creek Station discovered it, some miles from Fort Wallace, Kansas. Scalping, or pulling out the hair, the amputation of limbs and cutting, were rituals commonly practiced by the Indians on their victims in the belief that, even in the afterlife, a fallen warrior would be not retaliate.

The usual punishment for mild breaches of discipline was confinement, being assigned barrack tasks, among other punishments. In the photo titled 'Moral Session Horse' taken at Fort Brigger, Wyoming, the soldier remained in this position holding the heavy wooden sabre for a given time as punishment for having broken some rule.

chasing or stealing food, cultivating small gardens and hunting. After 1880, tinned food appeared, which facilitated the supply of food and led to an improvement in the diet.

Discipline

One of the most frequent problems for the officers was the enforcement of discipline. It was not unusual to find indulgent officers that permitted a relaxation of the rules, but when some limits were crossed, punishment could, at times, be excessive. If the offence was not serious, punishment was administered within the unit. Only the most grave cases were judged by a convened court martial.

Disease

Illnesses caused more deaths than combat itself. The poor food, contaminated water and, in general, the poor living conditions, combined with a lack of medical personnel and the low qualifications of the available medical staff increased the number of sick up to a tenth of each unit. Common illnesses were scurvy, dysentery, cholera and venereal diseases. The lack of adequate hygiene also contributed to the prolongation of these diseases.

The enemy's use of large calibre ammunition produced serious damage and the bullet wounds became easily infected and gangrenous, hence amputation was a common prac-

tice. Arrows were especially difficult and only a surgeon skilled in this type of wound could guarantee recovery. Another common accident was falling from horseback.

The 'Snowbirds' (1): Deserters

Desertion was rife, varying between 25% and 40% of the active troops annually. One of the reasons motivating this disloyal practice was the fact that the men had other opportunities to earn money during the winter months. Sometimes, desertion took place at crucial moments, such as on campaign against the Indians; hence it is understandable that many officers, like Custer, decided to order deserters to be shot, in order to warn others from doing the same.

(1) Nickname given to the deserters. It alluded to the migratory 'snowbirds' that only stayed in certain places during winter, sheltering from the harsh weather.

A long tiring journey awaited the new cavalry soldier before reaching his assigned unit. He generally began the trip by train to the station nearest his unit as far away as Dakota or Wyoming. From there he continued by whatever means available. This journey itself was a first adventure and he arrived at his post, somewhere on the Great Plains, tired, dirty and very hungry.

THE FORTS

During the first half of the 19th Century, the white man's settlements to the west of the Mississippi River were few and far between. From 1821 onwards, the fur trade established a series of commercial enclaves founded by the American Fur Company, dedicated to the purchase of buffalo and other animal furs from Indians, hunters and white trappers. They were usually constructed close to navigable rivers and the national flag hung from a tall pole in the centre, which, as well as indicating the location for many miles around, served to communicate certain signals by way of a previously agreed code. As the years passed, these buildings became an inevitable stopping point along the great routes, such as the Oregon Trail and the Bozeman Trail and, from 1865, many were sold to the army, given the decline of the fur trade and the military's need to occupy these territories. Many others were purpose built by the army and an extensive network of forts expanded throughout Indian Territory.

These forts contained the supplies for the soldiers whose mission it was to protect and subjugate the terri-

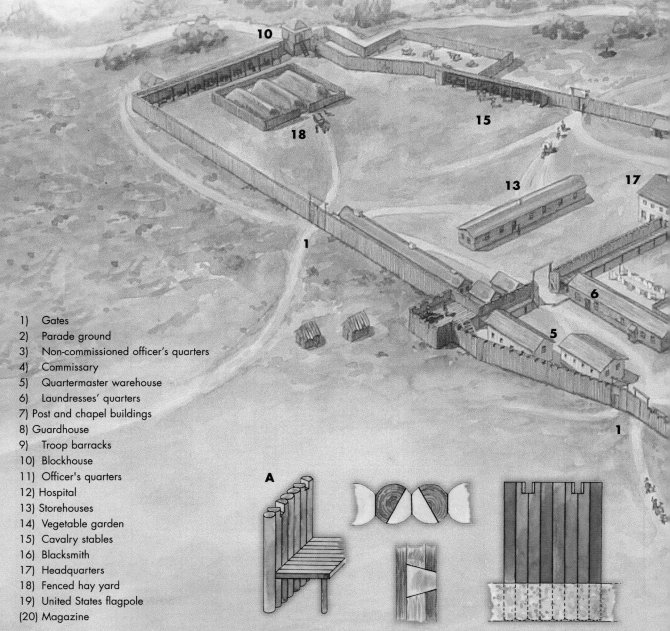

1) Gates
2) Parade ground
3) Non-commissioned officer's quarters
4) Commissary
5) Quartermaster warehouse
6) Laundresses' quarters
7) Post and chapel buildings
8) Guardhouse
9) Troop barracks
10) Blockhouse
11) Officer's quarters
12) Hospital
13) Storehouses
14) Vegetable garden
15) Cavalry stables
16) Blacksmith
17) Headquarters
18) Fenced hay yard
19) United States flagpole
(20) Magazine

tory. They also represented centres for provisioning and trade for the settlers, railroad and telegraph workers, miners and any curious Indian passing by wishing to do business. However, when the winds of war blew, their military activity was weak and these forts became general barracks and meeting and departure points for military campaigns.

These forts were built according to the importance of their position. Most were small, miserable frontier posts constructed from sun-dried bricks, with transitory occupation. Others reached a considerable scale with multiple wood or even stone buildings, according to the availability of materials in the zone. The more protected ones, so-called Stockade Forts, had a surrounding palisade and some even had defensive bastions.

However, in other areas, what were called Open Forts was constructed, with no defensive wall because, contrary to popular belief, Indians usually didn't attack forts because of the large number of casualties they sustained when doing so.

Fort Phil Kearney (Wyoming, 1866)

This fort was built by the army in just three months to protect the Bozeman Trail against frequent Indian attacks. It was surrounded by a palisade with two bastions at the ends. It also had all the necessary services and buildings for enduring an extended life on the Plains.

A – The palisade was usually built from trunks of wood about a foot thick (29'57 cm) embedded in the ground for about a third of their length. Loopholes were carved in the upper part. A raised passage was constructed against the inside of the palisade from which the fort surroundings could be surveyed and which also served as a firing platform.

THE CAVALRY UNIFORM

The cavalry soldiers of the Indian Wars era will always be remembered for their bright blue uniforms and yellow neckerchiefs although, in reality, the uniform varied greatly from this stereotypical image. The soldier's uniform was somewhat more 'personal' and the reasons for this are easily understandable: In the first instance, the isolation of the various forts inhibited contact between disparate units and delayed supplies. Secondly, the quality of the uniforms was very poor and didn't stand up to the harsh climate. During the Indian Wars, four uniform regulations were in service, corresponding to the years 1861,1872, 1882, and 1888, along with a number of uniform instructions called 'General Orders'. The surplus uniforms from the Civil War marked the first period of the Indian Wars, poorly finished clothing that had been produced in vast quantities. From 1872, the quality improved, but the new uniforms didn't reach all the garrisons and when they did, any attempt at harmonisation clashed with the individual soldiers' already embedded custom of dressing according to his preferences. While the stylised 'blue solders' were evident, they were mixed with a colourful blend of military clothing of different production date, complemented with items of clothing of civil and even Indian origin.

Most Commonly Used Army Issue Clothing

There were different types of army issue cavalry clothing, some more popular than others, according to their degree of comfort and functionality. Dark blue was used for jackets and overcoats, light blue for trousers. The cavalry's insignia colour was yellow, generally used to distinguish between different ranks and for other uniform adornments.

The frock coat was a superior item of clothing, used mostly by the officers, especially after the Civil War. It was made from cloth and had several rows of buttons, according to rank. Another item inherited from the Civil War was the cavalry combat jacket equipped with twelve buttons. By far the best and most commonly used item during the 25 years of the Indian Wars was the fatigue blouse. This came in several designs, according to the year of manufacture.

The trousers were sky blue, except for those of generals and General Staff officers, which were dark blue. The yellow stripe down the outer seam of the trousers was of different widths, 1.5 inches for officers, 1 inch for sergeants and 1/5 inch for corporals (1). The enlisted men had no stripe. Although the trousers were fitted with reinforcement in the area in contact with the saddle, they wore quickly and the troopers usually sewed a piece of white or plain coloured canvas as a replacement. There were several models of trousers, the basic difference being the presence of pockets, the form of the waist and fasteners.

The headdresses used were the forage cap, styled on the French quepis, and the campaign, or slouch hat. The latter was, as its name suggests, generally used on campaign because it was both comfortable and offered protection from the elements.

The riding boots were made of black leather and reached the knees.

During the winter, the light blue cape-overcoat was used, with an overlap that was buttoned at the chest and incorporated a cape that reached the elbows. Buffalo skin coats and others of lined canvas were also used against the extreme cold, although the latter were less effective at low temperatures.

For the more glamorous occasions, the cavalry soldier possessed an elegant full dress uniform of dark blue jacket trimmed in yellow over light blue trousers, with or without a yellow stripe according to rank. This uniform was made of a better quality material and also sported a Prussian-inspired spiked helmet with yellow cords and plume.

(1) The yellow strip on these trousers corresponds to the 1872 army issue, which was most commonly used during the Indian Wars. The American inch equals 254 mm.

Attack on the Pawnee people by elements of the 5th Cavalry in June 1869, on the banks of the South Platte River.

All the uniforms and equipment were of Civil War origin. The troopers are armed with Model 1860 percussion Army Colt revolvers, Model 1865 Spencer carbines and the 1860-model cavalry sabre.

Figure 1: Quartermaster-sergeant guidon-bearer from Company A, 5th Cavalry. Company guidons were borne by a non-commissioned officer. He wears a short twelve-buttoned army jacket, the waist ending in a small peak both at the front and back. It was yellow piped along the closure, collar, inside and the back. The neck had decorative buttonholes and two buttons. For greater comfort, the collar was either folded over or removed and the peaks at the waist were removed. NCO chevrons were worn on both arms. He wore a civilian shirt under the jacket. On his head he wears an 1864 Model Hardee hat made of black felt.

Figure 21: Private. He is dressed in a four-button fatigue blouse with the collars folded over and without pockets. The trousers, being the enlisted man's model, carried no yellow stripe down the seams. The hat is of the same type as in Fig. 1, but without any decoration.

Figure 3: Figure 3: Sergeant-bugler. This NCO sports the forage cap or kepi (from a contemporary French pattern), generally referred to as a 'bummer'. He wears a military jacket similar to that as the NCO in Fig.1, with the collars folded outwards. The trouser seams have a yellow stripe designated for sergeants.

LIFE IN THE FORT

The day at the fort began when the bugler sounded 'Reveille' at 6 a.m. and ended with the 'Retreat' call at 9 p.m. Between the two calls; the routine and unpopular barrack tasks were rotated.

In the cavalry units, one of the most important tasks was caring for the animals, which were cleaned and groomed daily. The stables were cleaned, and the animals fed three times daily with maize, oats and hay. The saddle, bridle and other horse furniture also required special attention, as all the items of equipment in the forts stores had to be maintained in a perfect state of repair.

During times of peace, the territory maintained relatively calm and excursions to collect fruit and hunt game were more common: deer, buffalo, wild boar, turkey and prairie dogs, as well as other animals were usually found in abundance on the Great Plains.

Social life and entertainment was conditioned by the isolated nature of the forts, with large distances between one fort and the next and often several days march to the nearest town. In this setting, spare time was spent with sporting activities such as baseball and horseracing though the most popular pastimes were card games (poker and faro were very popular) and the

consumption of alcohol, including whisky and other distilled drinks of dubious origin, such as Cactus Wine, Mule Skinner, Fire Water... the names give you stomach ache just reading them. Indeed, anything that served to get drunk and help forget for a while the dreaded sergeant and vicious Indians. The few soldiers who were not illiterate and were somewhat more sensitive spent their time reading and writing. Some, both troopers and officers, kept diaries and wrote notes with observations about nature and their experiences on the frontier.

Contact with women was rare. The few who lived at the fort, excluding from the officers wives, were cooks and laundresses hired by the army and many of them maintained intimate relations with the soldiers. The Indian women, commonly called 'squaws', usually visit-

ed the forts during times of peace and it was hardly surprising that some of them had mixed race children.

Compared to civilian occupations, the monthly wages were miserly: $13 for an enlisted man up to $22 for a sergeant, if it arrived and that could be very seldom. Even when it did, it didn't go very far and evaporated quickly in the fort shops or in the pockets of the frontier's travelling salesmen. The habit of visiting the ''Old West' Saloons, gambling and drinking houses (that, often, were little more than brothels) and being absent from duty was, understandably, quite a serious affair. More often than not, when an important campaign was envisaged, the monthly pay parade was usually postponed until the columns had left the fort, thus avoiding these temptations.

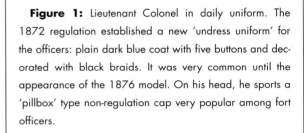

Figure 1: Lieutenant Colonel in daily uniform. The 1872 regulation established a new 'undress uniform' for the officers: plain dark blue coat with five buttons and decorated with black braids. It was very common until the appearance of the 1876 model. On his head, he sports a 'pillbox' type non-regulation cap very popular among fort officers.

Figure 2: Saddler Sergeant in full dress uniform. In accordance with the 1872 ruling, a Prussian style dress uniform was adopted. The NCOs and troopers wore jackets with a single row of buttons, yellow shoulder boards and yellow neck patches upon which the regiment number was marked. The most significant item of clothing was the felt-lined Prussian-style helmet crowned with a bright yellow-dyed horsehair plume.

The officers dress uniform was a double-breasted frock-coat (with two rows of seven buttons for lieutenants and captains and two rows of nine for the higher ranked officers), and shoulder boards on which the regimental number and the officers rank was indicated.

Figure 3 and 4: Privates at the fort. Fig. 3 wears an 1877 model grey flannel regulation shirt with just three buttons and open at the chest, and a 1872 model cap, commonly used at fort. Fig. 4 wears a civilian checked shirt that was very popular and was normally of higher quality than the army issue ones. Both troopers wear the regulation white elastic braces to hold up their trousers (usually made of cotton) fastened with buttons.

THE HARSH WINTERS

The Great Plains can be quite inhospitable, especially in winter, when temperatures can drop below -20°C in some places. Although the climate is dry for the greater part of the year and sunny days are abundant, the weather can change suddenly due to the presence of strong winds capable of generating snowstorms in a question of minutes. The thermometer can drop rapidly and a man without adequate warm clothing can quickly freeze to death.

With the arrival of the cold winter months, campaigning on the Great Plains declined notably. The Indians settled in their winter camps in sites protected from the harsh weather and well stocked with food. Their great horse herds didn't have the strength to undertake long journeys, due to the difficulty of finding adequate pasture. The soldiers were also confined to their forts, many of which were located in very open, cold places where it was essential to dress warmly in order to endure the long guard duties and life in general in the open air. At times, the general headquarters staff took the decision to take action during the snowy season. As the Indians were also, to a great extent, very limited in terms of mobility, they could more easily be trapped and attacked during the winter months. However, the 'blue soldiers' had to find better clothing for riding in search of hostile camps during these forays.

The light blue cape-overcoat also incorporated a short cape or cloak, which reached the waist. It was totally inadequate for enduring the low temperatures in the Indian territories: It neither protected against the sub-zero winds, nor was completely impermeable. Attempts were made to improve its properties by lining it with grey army-issue blankets or lining the inside with dry plants as a means of creating a heat insulation layer. In 1876, the army, in an attempt to find a better solution, purchased buffalo skin coats. These were both expensive and of insufficient quantity, hence another, cheaper type of coat was commissioned made from canvas and lined with various materials.

The manufacture of other accessories to combat the cold was also undertaken, including hats and gloves. At first, they were made from buffalo skin but these performed badly. However, others made of rat and other rodent skins were found to be both more comfortable and practical.

For long rides on horseback, during which the extremities became numb with cold, numerous ideas were looked at which resulted in some strange clothing being tried out: cork soles for the feet, wooden flip-flops fixed to the boots, long buffalos skin leggings that covered the knees and an assortment of other improvisations. However, the majority of these ''improvements' proved useless against the cold when riding.

North Dakota, winter 1884.

Figure 1: This private wears an 1883 model overcoat. They were made from thick canvas and lined on the inside with blankets. More expensive variants were made from lambskin. They were less effective against the cold than buffalo hide. Several types existed, with different buttons patterns, although they all had high collars to protect the neck and were fastened at the waist with a belt. They were known by the name of their place of manufacture: Saint Paul (Minnesota). This trooper is also equipped with a buffalo hide cap complete with visor and earflaps that could be folded outwards and tied on the top of the cap. They were manufactured from 1877 onwards. He is armed with a Model 1873 Springfield carbine.

Figure 2: This private wears a buffalo hide overcoat, manufactured from 1877 onwards. It was the finest item of clothing of which a soldier could equip himself against the bitter cold of the Great Plains. Many companies used their own personal expense accounts to purchase this type of overcoat and they were shared among the men when on watch during the winter months. The trooper is also equipped with canvas and buffalo skin boots with fur on the inside. While these were very warm, they were useless for horse riding. On his head he wears a rat skin cap, while on his hands he has sealskin gloves, manufactured in the 1880s as a substitute for buffalo hide. He is armed with an 1873 model Springfield carbine along with an 1873 model Single-Action Army Colt revolver.

Figure 3: This Sergeant Major wears a cape-overcoat, the sole item of army issue winter clothing before 1873, which continued to be produced for many years with slight modifications. It was light blue with an inner lining of the same colour, except for models produced after 1880 where the lining was yellow. The NCOs wore rank cheuvrons reaching the knuckles, thus making them visible while wearing the cape. The officers could also use a cape-overcoat very similar to this one, but dark blue in colour and with plaited cords of black silk.

ORGANISING THE CAVALRY

The Cavalry Regiments (1)

The basic cavalry unit in 1865 remained the regiment that, in theory, was commanded by a colonel. However, command was often designated to the General Staff with operational command being assigned to the lieutenant colonel. According to the 1861 regulation, a regiment comprised 12 companies (2) that tended to be grouped into four battalions of two or three companies each, normally commanded by a major. Each company could be divided into two squadrons (3), led by a lieutenant. In practice, smaller groups within the squadron could be delimited, commanded by NCOs and these subdivisions were occasionally called squads as in the infantry unit style.

Dispersal along the Frontier

During the war with the Redskins, attempts were made to control a very extended territory hence cavalry units were spread out along a very wide front. In 1868, for example, 80 cavalry companies were dispersed in 60 forts, but they were incapable of carrying out a better level of prevention and protection as was intended.

This dispersion had two unfortunate consequences in the fight against the Indians, highlighted perfectly in the attempt at protecting the Bozeman Trail. This important route provided access from the east to the gold mines near the cities of Virginia and Helena. It left Wyoming territory northwards and passed through Montana and across the best hunting grounds of the

'Cavalry Charge on the Southern Plains', by Frederick Remington.
The uniting of the whole cavalry regiment and their use as an operational unit was very rare and limited to the great campaigns. As a consequence, a group spirit, habitual under other circumstances, rarely formed.

7th Cavalry NCOs as part of an historical re-enactment group. The 7th Cavalry also fell victim to the dispersion of the companies across different forts and, from its creation in 1866; Custer only managed to unite his whole regiment during the Little Bighorn campaign.

Sioux, Cheyenne and Arapahoe tribes. A chain of forts were established to protect the trail: Fort Laramie, Fort Reno, Fort Phil Kearny and Fort Smith, with distances of 161 km (100 miles), 108 km (67 miles) and 146 km (90 miles) between them, respectively. Only a few companies from the 2nd Cavalry and some scarce infantry units protected the whole route; each group lacked the mobility and strength to mutually assist each other in times of need. So, it was understandable that Red Cloud, the great Sioux Chief, and his 3,000 warriors, with the ability to move with great speed, were able to cut off the important route and maintain all the forts under siege, spreading panic throughout the whole territory.

The Cavalry Company

The widespread dispersion of the regiments in companies along the frontier meant that the basic administrative and operational unit were the companies themselves. Each one was commanded by a captain identified by a letter from 'A' to 'M'. This denomination defined 13 companies within the same regiment; but the letter 'J' was not used, to avoid confusion with the letter 'I' (due to the similar way in which they are written) and with the letter 'A' (because of the similar pronunciation in English). The twelve remaining letters were left for 12 theoretical companies, according to the 1861 regulation.

The Soldiers Force

The numerical strength of the cavalry regiments and companies varied substantially throughout the Indian Wars. In 1865, the theoretical effective regimental strength was 997 soldiers and officers and 96 for each company. By 1869, government cutbacks had already officially reduced these numbers, setting them at 60 men for a company and limiting the number of its NCOs. It was only after the disaster at Little Bighorn in

1876 that the effective strength was again increased, reaching a maximum of 100 men per company.

However, the cavalry's problems did not only originate from the Washington cutbacks. Desertion and illness was commonplace and it was not unusual for a unit to rely on just half its theoretical affective strength. This weakness affected both the troops and the officers, the latter even more so, as many of them were seconded to the Regimental General Staff or even the Army General Staff in the case of larger units.

(1) The American terminology is used to avoid confusion.

(2) The term 'troop' was frequently used from 1880, referring to the companies.

(3) The unit termed 'squadron' could lead to confusion, hence it was decided to use the more usual operational structure of the time. As indicated above, the term 'squadron' was normally used to describe a unit directly below that of a company and was the equivalent of an infantry platoon. In contrast, and also appearing in the 1861 Regulation, reference was occasionally made of a squadron composed of two companies.

THE CAVALRY REGIMENTS

1st Cavalry. Originally the 1st Regiment of Dragoons, it acquired this new denomination from 1861. It operated alternatively in Oregon, Arizona and Montana, and mainly confronted the Crow, Cheyenne, Apache, Nez Percé and Bannock tribes.

2nd Cavalry. It was called the 2nd Regiment of Dragoons until 1861. It operated across Wyoming, Kansas and Montana. It fought during the Little Bighorn campaign and in the wars against the Nez Percé and Bannock Indians.

3rd Cavalry. Until 1861, they were called Mounted Riflemen. They fought the Cheyenne, Ute and Comanche on the plains of Texas, New Mexico and Arizona and also took part in the Little Bighorn campaign.

4th Cavalry. It was originally formed as the 1st Cavalry Regiment and adopted its new name in 1861. Led by Colonel Mackenzie, a distinguished cavalry commander, it played an important role in the Indian Wars. It served from 1865 to 1876 on the Central Plains, fighting the Cheyenne, Comanche and Sioux. It participated in the Little Bighorn campaign and also fought against the Apache in New Mexico.

5th Cavalry. It was founded as the 2nd Cavalry and changed its name in 1861. It was one of the regiments that played the greatest role in the Indian Wars, fighting the Sioux, Cheyenne, Comanche, Nez Percé and Apache tribes. It took part in the Little Bighorn campaign.

6th Cavalry. It was originally founded as the 3rd Cavalry and received its new name in 1861. It served on the Great Plains from 1871 to 1874 and 1884 to 1891 and on the Pine Ridge campaign against the Sioux.

7th Cavalry. It was formed in 1866 and served without relief from its creation. It was the most famous cavalry regiment, thanks to its charismatic leader George Armstrong Custer and its partial and legendary destruction at Little Bighorn. It was also responsible for the slaughter of the Cheyenne people in the Washita River and took part in other campaigns such as Pine Ridge and the Battle of Wounded Knee.

8th Cavalry. Since its foundation in 1866, it served spasmodically in various Great Plains actions, including the Pine Ridge campaign.

9th Cavalry. It was created in 1866 and was composed entirely of black soldiers, except for the officers. It served on the Great Plains from 1876 to 1891 against the Apache, and during the Pine Ridge campaign.

10th Cavalry. It was the second regiment composed of Afro-Americans and was formed in 1866. Until 1872 it intervened against the Cheyenne, Apache, Kiowa and Comanche, returning to action in 1877 and 1878 serving in the south of the Great Plains.

REGIMENT COMMAND STRUCTURE

Field Officers: Regiment or Battalion Leaders.
1 Colonel
1 Lieutenant-Colonel
3 Major

Staff Officers: Officers in charge of logistic and administrative tasks and other regimental level specialisations.
1 Adjutant Officer (generally a lieutenant responsible for administration)
2 Quartermaster and Commissary Officers
1-2 Surgeon Officers
2 Chief Buglers

Non-commissioned Officers (N.C.O.) and Enlisted Men
1 Sergeant-Major
1 Quartermaster-Sergeant
1 Commissary-Sergeant
1 Saddler Sergeant
1 Veterinary Sergeant
1 Chief-trumpeter
1 Farrier
2 Regimental Hospital Steward
16 Musicians

COMPANY COMMAND STRUCTURE

Line Officers: company or squadron leaders
1 Captain (A)
1 1st Lieutenant (B)
1 2nd Lieutenant (C)

Non-commissioned Officers and Enlisted Men
1 First Sergeant (D)
1 Quartermaster-Sergeant (E)
1 Commissary Sergeant (F)
1 Saddler Sergeant (G)
5 Sergeants (H)
8 Corporals (I)
2 Musicians (generally buglers) (J)
2 Wagoners
2 Farriers (1 of them: K)
78 Privates

FLAGS AND INSIGNIA

1. Commissioned Officers (COs)

The commissioned officers wore shoulder-straps piped with the yellow of the cavalry. They were either embroidered or printed in tin and carried symbols of rank on the inside. They also wore rank insignia on coat and overcoat collars.

2. Non-commissioned Officers (NCOs)

The non-commissioned officers wore large yellow chevrons on both the combat jacket and overcoat sleeves, indicating their respective ranks and specialisations.

3. Flags and guidons

Each company had its own identifying guidon. From 1862 to 1885, the colours of the American flag with the stars and stripes were adopted, adding the company's letter (3a). The standard was carried by a Guidon Bearer who was normally a non-commissioned officer. From 1885, a red and white bicoloured guidon was adopted, also showing the company and regiment signs (3b). General Custer had his own personal red and blue guidon with two crossed sabres (3c).

Each cavalry regiment also had its own regimental flag with the Arms of the United States embroidered in silk, including the famous American eagle with its wings outstretched and the Latin phrase E Pluribus Unum. The background was usually blue. However, the 10th Regiment was the exception, as shown in the illustration, as it was yellow (3d).

4 Campaign Caps and Hats.

4.1 The cap used was a similar to the so-called *quepis*

1

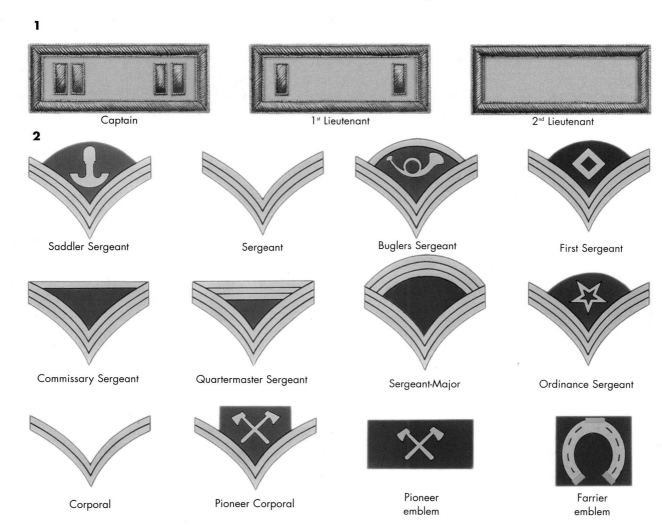

| Captain | 1st Lieutenant | 2nd Lieutenant |

2

Saddler Sergeant   Sergeant   Buglers Sergeant   First Sergeant

Commissary Sergeant   Quartermaster Sergeant   Sergeant-Major   Ordinance Sergeant

Corporal   Pioneer Corporal   Pioneer emblem   Farrier emblem

of French origin (4a). They were normally only used in the fort, as they quickly became saturated when it rained and offered no protection to the neck from the blazing sun. The models inherited from the Civil War were known by their nickname 'bummer', a later version improved upon this with the 1872 model shown in the illustration.

4.2 The first hat emanated from the Civil War and was known as the 'Hardee' or Model 1858 Dress Hat, made of black felt (4b). It had a yellow cord finished with two tassels for the NCOs and troopers. For the officers, this cord was golden and black, or just the latter colour, depending on the rank and finished with two decorations in the shape of acorns. Theoretically, it also had one decorative feather for the troops and two for the NCOs. It was in use until 1872, but was normally used without any of the previously mentioned decorations. Later, another hat model was produced, the '1872-pattern folding hat', with wider flaps that could be gathered together at the upper part thanks to

a hook fixed to the upper part of the hat, thus completely changing its appearance such that it looked more like the typical French hat chapeau-de-bras. This model was very unpopular and from 1875 others based on the civilian 'East Coast' model with ventilation holes were manufactured. In spite of all the attempts at improving the headdress, civilian hats were always preferred and straw hats were used in hot climates and during warm weather.

4.3 The crossed sabres have been the United Stated Cavalry coat of arms since 1851 (4c). In theory, campaign hats and caps usually carried this symbol together with the regiment and company numbers (depending on uniform regulations applied). These symbols were made of tin for the troops and embroidered on a black patch for the officers (the crossed sabres were yellow with the regiment number in silver). It is not uncommon to find contemporary photographs showing hats without any decoration or distinctive marking.

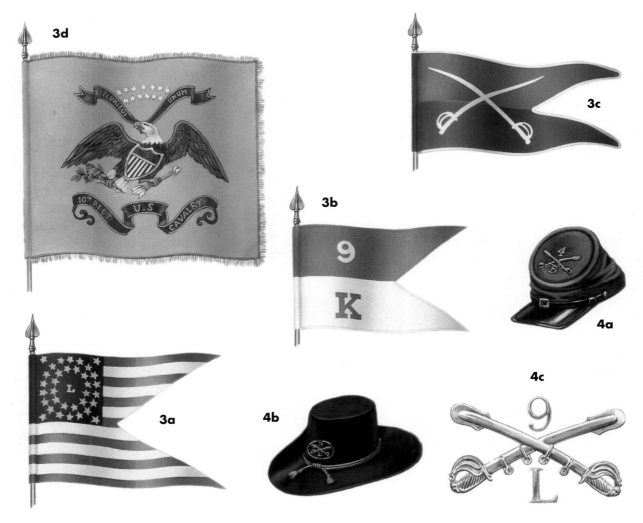

STRATEGY AND TACTICS DURING THE INDIAN WARS

Strategy

The American Indians were principally nomadic hunters, who had great capacity for movement thanks to their great herds of horses. They usually attacked independently, or in small groups of dozens or, sometimes, hundreds of warriors.

Fighting this elusive enemy was a difficult. There were no important objectives, no lines of communication and supply and no great destructive battles. The Indians attacked a hundred times and retreated on just as many other occasions, usually without loss, as if the land had opened up and swallowed them. By 1865, the frontier had became an ever more unsafe place and a small fort along the eastern boundary could not solve the problem.

Strategy had to be reviewed and the initiative regained. This was achieved by forming strong colums enough to hold out in hostile territories without fear of Indian attacks, then locate their villages and destroy them. To this end, great campaigns were planned and initiated where large military groups left far apart forts in convergent directions to surround the enemy, even running into him along the march. The main problem was that this network was not sufficiently dense in order to cover such extensive territories and the Indian populations could usually move much faster than the slow but essential baggage and supply trains of the soldiers. To solve this problem, each group relied on cavalry units of greater mobility. These fulfilled the functions of scouting, harassing and locating the most important enemy.

An example of this type of operation was General Hancock's 1867 campaign. The expedition covered more than 1,000 miles without ever coming into contact with a single Cheyenne or Sioux Indian while they, meanwhile, spread panic throughout Kansas, constantly laughing at the soldiers. Undoubtedly, the Indians were too skilful and mobile, the territories too large and the army officers too inexperienced.

General Sheridan, an intelligent, thinking officer, concluded that offensive operations could only be carried out when the Indian camps were immobile: in their winter villages, blocked by the snow. In contrast, the army was still able to carry out its re-supply missions whenever necessary, even during the most harsh winter conditions. This type of campaign was an immediate success and, in the

Painting of a cavalry charge by Frederick Remington The cavalry column broke and reformed into one or more lines, thus presenting a larger battlefront. The horses were advanced at a trot, nervously awaiting the order to gallop and then the final charge. This type of charge obtained the best results against fixed targets, such as villages, where its effect was devastating.

winter of 1868, Custer massacred Black Kettle's peaceful Cheyenne band without a thought on the banks of the Washita River. The strategy of these attacks, while efficient, was ruthless and devastating. It marked the beginning of the end of Indian independence.

Cavalry Tactics

The U.S. cavalry's tactical doctrine was defined in the 1867 manual, written by the officer Emory Upton. It was based on his experiences during the Civil War and, unfortunately, was not a great help against the Red skins. Notwithstanding, it established certain principles that remained valid.

The Charge

The cavalry's manoeuvre of excellence was the charge. It had a destructive and sudden effect that could break a defence, annihilate and cause the enemy to flee, to be later massacred during the following pursuit. On the majority of occasions, the charge rapidly dispersed the Indians, as they feared direct confrontations with cavalry units, because of their greater firing power. The cavalry unit was small and, if split up during the pursuit of hostile groups, they ran the risk of falling into ambushes that could have fatal consequences for the Long Knives.

The Firing Line

Contrary to popular belief, the cavalry deployed dismounted on many occasions, mainly due to the fact that firing effectively from horseback was very difficult and the rider/mount target presented to the enemy was quite large. The cavalrymen quickly learned that the best way to save his horse was to rely on his greater fire power: 'If you are within range of the Indians, stop, dismount, open fire and keep them in line'. Riding in front of Redskins meant almost certain death.

When coming into contact with hostiles, the soldiers dismounted and spread out along the ground and opened fire with carbines and revolvers. The lines of shooters were in open order with a few metres between each man, while one in four took care of the horses. These combat lines could be either one or several deep. In the most desperate cases, a barricade was improvised with whatever could be found: carriages, saddles and fallen horses. With the adoption of the Springfield carbine in 1873, successive waves of Indians were repulsed more easily, as occurred in the Wagon Box Fight. This was as in spite of the fact that it was a single shot, breech-loading weapon and, although it was not as efficient at the Spencer or Winchester-style repeating rifles did, it was more powerful, had a greater effective range and was more accurate.

Marching Columns

Large military column marches that covered vast distances across hostile territory were frequent and had their own particular advancing technique. In the van, two groups advanced at 450m (408 yards) and 750m (682 yards) from the bulk of the column. At the rear and flanks, other detached groups were sent out, such that a protective screen warned of and protected against any attempt at attack. The cavalry was the ideal weapon for this task. The settler wagon trains and supply convoys could also adopt this tactic and it could also be used to protect the teams of railroad workers although, on these occasions, the afforded protection was usually inferior.

1. Attacking in Lines.
The company deployed spread out and waited for the order to charge. This was first initiated at the trot for the first 40m, changing into the long trot for 25m (23 yards) and, finally, into the full galloping charge for 45 or 70 m (41 or 64 yards).

2: Attacking in Column.
If the enemy were well positioned, the charge-in-line abreast would not have enough continuity and impact. In these circumstances, the cavalry could decide to charge in a column formation. However, the disadvantage of doing this was that the flanks were left exposed; hence two parallel attacking columns were more commonly used.

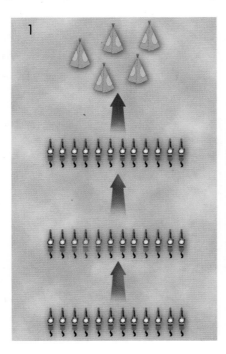
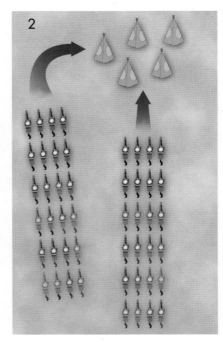

THE ELUSIVE INDIAN: SKIRMISHES AND AMBUSHES

The Indian Wars were primarily characterised by hundreds of small confrontations occurring during quick incursions and ambushes: A guerrilla war in which Indian groups attacked settler's camps, military supply convoys, railways, stagecoach routes, telegraph installations and any other of the white man's interests.

While the Indians vigorously defended their territory and way of life from the invader, their attacks never conformed to any strategy neither did they know how to take advantage of a tactical victory. The reasons for this were simple: As a nomadic people, they had no conception of strategic territorial control and their fragmentation into rival tribes and small groups rarely facilitated a coordinated attack involving thousands of warriors.

The cavalry soldier fought individualist warriors, who understood conflict as a natural event and part of their culture. For the Redskins, fighting was as natural and daily an event as hunting buffalo and they had been taught this since birth. They never managed to understand the mentality of the whasichu (1), those soldiers who pursued them inexorably wherever they were, destroying their camps and pony herds.

War meant glory and honour and after having demonstrated their worth before the enemy and carrying out a scalping, they fled in good humour to celebrate their victory without stopping to ask themselves what the white man would do the following day.

The 'blue soldiers' could inflict a large number of losses, hence the Indians avoided direct conflict with cavalry units and focused their efforts on attacking small patrols and convoys. When a fort sent for reinforcements, they often arrived too late and the relieving contingent often found their comrades already dead. On more fortunate occasions, the reinforcements managed to arrive in time and chased off the Indians, who usually disappeared without a trace. Sometimes, it was all part of a trick and the soldiers were led to a place where they were ambushed and massacred. The most daring cavalry officers accepted the chase aware of the risks involved, sometimes purely due to an accumulated sense of impotence and an abiding confidence in their superior fire power, other times because of an ingrained sense of superiority when faced with the 'uncivilised and savage Indians'. However, disaster struck when daring became arrogant stu-

pidity, as happened to Captain Fetterman when he left Fort Phil Kearny to help a 'firewood train': It was he who had boldly stated, *'Give me 80 men and I'll cut through the entire Sioux Nation'*. This reckless officer was later found with his eighty men, scalped and terribly mutilated.

Witnesses from the reinforcements that arrived too late to help their comrades were appalled by the savagery of the Indians. Horrified, one man related: *'Here and there we saw strange white marks that turned out to be the bodies of naked soldiers. Eyes were pulled out and left on the rocks, noses and ears were cut off, jaw bones and teeth were extracted, feet and arms were cut off, genitals were sliced, orifices were penetrated with spears and arrows, skulls were cut open and intestines were extracted and left exposed around the bodies...'* The hatred that the Indians felt for the 'long knives' was such that they stripped and mutilated the bodies in the belief that the dead men's spirits would be both helpless and disfigured and the soldiers could never return to the kingdom that awaited each warrior after death in combat. In many instances, fear of the treatment meted out by the Indians was so great that some committed suicide moments before being captured by the Indians. However, they were not all capable of killing themselves and when they surrendered, they were scorned by the Indians, who left them in the hands of women and teenagers to finish off as a sign of contempt. In contrast, if a soldier demonstrated uncommon bravery, he was spared from such a savage practice.

(1) Name with which the Indians called the white man. It had negative connotations and came to mean 'greedy'.

Apache ambush on a cavalry unit supply convoy, Arizona 1882.

For the Indian tribes, attacks were also carried out for economic reasons, as they took possession of any horses, weapons, ammunition and other consumer goods such as sugar, coffee, liquor and other foodstuffs common to the white man.

The soldiers are armed with Springfield 1873 carbines and Colt 45 revolvers and are wearing the dark blue shirts adopted from 1881 onwards.

CAVALRY WEAPONS

In 1865, the individual cavalryman's armoury consisted of a sabre, pistol and carbine. Once the Civil War had ended, a chaotic assortment of weaponry became available that was used in the Indian Wars until 1873. With the arrival of the metal cartridge with the bullet, gunpowder and percussion cap incorporated, a new generation of weapons was born and its standardisation began.

The Sabre

This weapon, the cavalry units' symbol of excellence, was in steep decline. During the Civil War, the Confederates had practically ceased using them. The vast open spaces of the American West and the Indian warrior's respect for hand-to-hand combat favoured even more the preference for firearms. The model used in the Indian Wars was the same as that used during the Civil War, fundamentally the 1860 curved blade model.

The Revolver

After the defeat of the Confederate States, the cavalry inherited an assortment of percussion revolvers of the 'cap and ball' type. These were slow and complicated to reload, as they used paper cartridges that only included the gunpowder and bullet and it was necessary to separately add the percussion cap for ignition. The most common were the Colt Navy .36 calibre (1), the Colt Army and the Remington Army, both .44 calibres. They were all single action revolvers. (2). Given the slowness of reloading, several pre-charged cylinders were carried, and even two or more ready-charged revolvers in the waistband. This type of cap and ball weapon was unreliable: The paper cartridge was often broken, it had to be kept dry and the hammer sometimes fired several cartridges at the same time. Because of these flaws, it was a rare gun that could manage to fire its six shots. Moreover, these revolvers were only effective at short range, although their large calibre meant that they had a high stopping power, which resulted in terrible wounds.

From 1871, the army tried out new models from Colt, Remington, Webley and Tranter. They all displayed significant improvements as they all utilised the new metal cartridge that could be loaded at the rear of the cylinder. However, for the time being, the single

1873 Model Single-Action Army Colt. It was the army issue weapon from 1873 and cost just $13 as the great U.S. steel works produced high quality steel at a low price and the mechanised production-line manufacturing process kept the cost down. Civilian versions were also manufactured and these became very popular and were given various nicknames, including 'Widow maker', Peacemaker' and 'Equalizer'. It was an efficient, rugged weapon, although it lacked a reliable safety lock between the cartridge percussion cap and the hammer. This meant that commonly it was loaded with just five cartridges with the hammer resting on the empty chamber.

The efficiency of the Springfield carbine was such that a dismounted firing line could hold off hoards of Indians even when outnumbered.

action system was preferred and continued in use due to its simpler, more reliable mechanism. Finally, in 1873, the cavalry adopted the Colt .45 Single Action Army model. This proved to be a robust, efficient weapon that had been subjected to hard tests by military technicians, from which it emerged successfully.

The Carbine

The carbine differs from a rifle in that it is shorter and is somewhat less powerful with a shorter range, due to its shorter barrel, and is less accurate mainly due to the distance between the eye and the sight. However, that said, it was an ideal weapon for the cavalry because it was lighter and easier to carry.

The primary carbines inherited from the Civil War were the Sharp, Spencer, Springfield and Remington models, all breech loading. Among them, the Spencer stands out; it was a very popular repeating weapon before 1873, but it usually jammed and hence many soldiers placed their trust in the Sharp more, even though it was slower to fire.

In 1870, the army decided to try out a new rifle and carbine and thus standardise weapons and calibres. The Erskine S. Allin model breechblock was chosen, to avoid paying manufacturing rights again. Numerous weapons were tested and, finally, the Springfield was selected. A repeating weapon was specifically not chosen as it was felt they possessed insufficient power, range and precision. The decision was not without its detractors and many officers, like the experienced Major Ronald Mackenzie of the 4ᵗʰ Cavalry, applied for Winchester-type repeating carbines as they valued

its firing ratio as being decisive when confronting the Indians.

With a few modifications, the 1873 model Springfield remained in use until 1890. It had an effective range of between 460 and 550m (503 and 601 yards), but the usual firing distance was between 140 and 275m (128 and 251 yards). It had some jamming problems, but these were usually attributable to the ammunition, as the ductile copper sheaths were easily deformed when fired, making extraction difficult. Another problem, also derived from the cartridges, was that the leather became covered in green and other dirt caused by the ammunition that, given the high temperatures resulting from firing, caused them to stick to the sheath.

Many officers purchased revolvers, carbines and rifles privately; there was even an improved version of the Springfield carbine destined for these customers. Long-range rifles were also used, mostly for hunting purposes. These acquisitions were prohibited for the NCOs and enlisted men, though this rule was probably often broken.

(1) Hundredths of an American inch (9,1mm).

(2) In order to turn the cylinder on these single-action type revolvers, it was first necessary to draw back the hammer with the thumb. On the double-action models, the cylinder turned with the simple application of pressure on the trigger.

1. Belts

Black leather belt with a steel buckle (1a). This final one remained in use until 1881, when it became authorised for officers only. From the waist hangs the 'cap box' (1b), a small cartridge holder for storing the copper percussion caps for 'cap and ball' type revolvers and that later continued to be used to hold cartridge ammunition. Different models of holster existed for the revolver (1c); the model shown in the illustration was designed for the 'cap and ball' type. In practice, both open or closed, i.e. with closure flap, holsters were employed.

With the introduction of the metal cartridge, various types of belts incorporating cartridge loops to hold the ammunition were adopted (1d). The leather bullet belt was already in existence in 1866, but the troops didn't like it and it was normally replaced with civilian models. In 1876, the production of 30,000 belts with built-in canvas cartridge belts was commissioned. Several models existed, with different production years. The most popular ones were the so-called 'Prairie Belt', 'Christian' and the 'Mills'; the latter is shown in the illustration and already incorporates the new H-shaped buckle used from 1881 (1e).

2. 1860 Model Sabre

It was a slightly curved sabre, based on French models. It had a steel guard and leather grip. The scabbard was also made of steel. High-ranking officers were entitled to carry different models. Custer used a heavier double-edged sabre for some time, taken from a Confederate officer who he had pursued and killed; it had a nice legend engraved on it in Spanish: *'No me saques sin razón, no me envaines sin honor'* ('Draw me not without reason, sheath me not without honour')

3. Knives

They were more of an all-purpose utensil rather than a weapon, very useful for unblocking weapons. The legendary 'Bowie knife' was made in the U.K. and was acquired by soldiers using their own funds (3a). The first Army Issue one was the 1880 campaign model knife (3b).

4. Indian Production

It was not unusual for soldiers to use weapons made or decorated by the Indians. Here, a knife sheath (4a) and holster (4b) are shown.

5. 1851 Model Percussion Navy Colt

This was a .36 calibre 'cap and ball' type revolver. This weapon, and its brother the Colt Army, had the upper part of the frame open. While this made the weapon less robust and accurate, it reduced the accumulation of percussion cap and gunpowder residue making the revolving cylinder mechanism less prone to blockage.

6. 1860 Model Percussion Army Colt

This was a 'cap and ball' revolver frequently used after

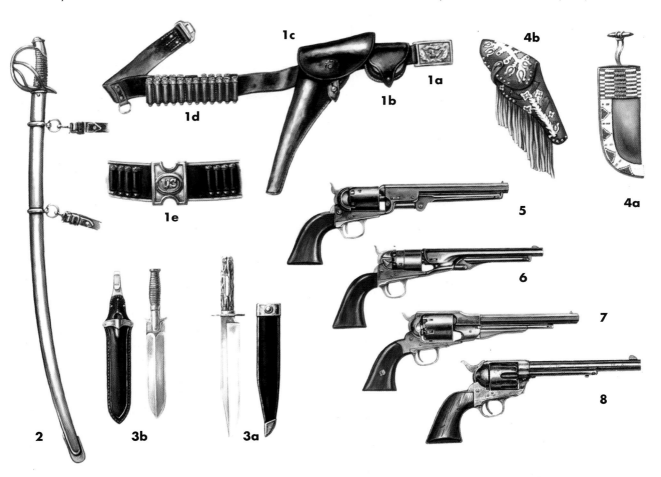

the Civil War. It was .44 calibre, which gave it greater stopping power and was preferred by the cavalry over the Navy model. A version modified for use with jacketed cartridges appeared later.

7. 1858 Model Percussion Remington
.44 calibre 'cap and ball' type revolver with a more rugged frame than the previous models.

8. 1873 Model Single-Action Army Colt
Its 7 inch barrel (177 mm) and .45 calibre 'centre fire' type cartridge (1) provided it with a high level of efficiency and stopping power. Its solid frame design and walnut grips made it robust and reliable.

9. Sharp Carbine
.52 calibre carbine with a linen or paper capsule. Its main virtue was the safety of the firing mechanism, which stemmed from its simplicity.

10. 1865 Model Spencer Carbine
It was a .52 calibre repeating carbine. It used metal cartridges that were introduced seven at a time into a tube with a loading spring through the butt (10a). It had a special cartridge holder, called the 'Blakeslee', which contained ten tubes of seven bullets (10b). To store metal cartridges, another types of cartridge holder were modified, such as this one originally designed for the infantry and adapted to carry .50 calibre cartridges (10c).

11. 1873 Model U.S. Springfield Carbine
This was a 45/70 calibre breech-loading Allin breechblock carbine (2) popularly known as the 'Trapdoor'. It had a barrel measuring 22 inches (55,8 cm) and was the cavalry's basic weapon from its introduction until 1890.

12. Carbine sling
Used for all types of carbines

13. Gatling gun
This was a 45/70 calibre machine gun adopted by the U.S. Army in 1866. Its firing mechanism was based on a multi-tube cylinder (the number of barrels varied according to the model) triggered by a crank. It could fire up to 200 shots per minute. Although it was taken on some campaigns during the Indian Wars, it was neither useful nor popular among the men who hated having to drag these slow contraptions.

(1) 'Central fire or 'rim fire' referred to the place where percussion occurred on the cartridge.

(2) In North American weapons of the time, the gunpowder charge contained in the cartridge was usually indicated following the calibre. It was measured in grains, the equivalent in the decimal system is: 1 grain = 0.0648 grammes.

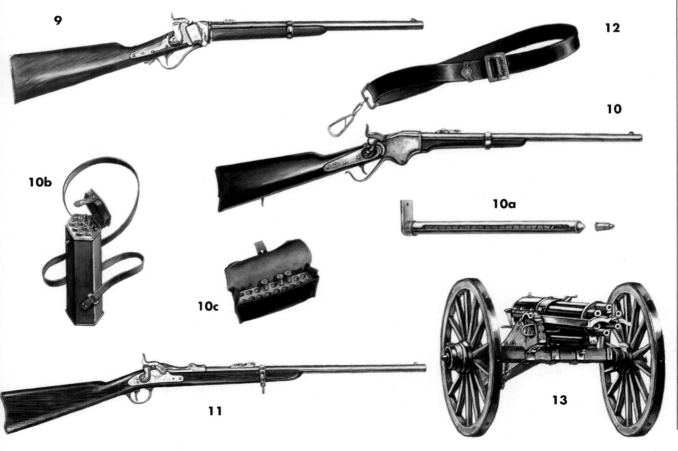

THE HORSES

There are few places on the planet as appropriate for the use of horses as the vast North American plains. The indigenous people rapidly adopted them following their introduction on the continent by the Spanish. They rode rugged, agile ponies, which transformed them into fearsome warriors. It was not an unjustified assumption by many that the Plains Indians were considered to be the best light cavalry in the world. Their opponents, those regiments of U.S. cavalry were equally dependent on their mounts to be able to confront such a fearful enemy. The horse was both the spirit and engine of the Indian Wars.

The selection of army horses was usually conducted by a military committee that visited determined ranches and selected the most suitable animals for the army, according to certain features and the budget. The army purchasers selected healthy equines that had already been broken and weighing between 408 and 499 kilos (900 to 1100 pounds) with a height of 15 hands (144 cm). Analysis of contemporary photographs reveals that the quality of horses varied considerably, given the budgetary constraints and the corruption of civil servants and suppliers (as was usual in all army supply areas). The most common coat colour was sorrel, bay and chestnut and, to a lesser degree, black and grey.

During the 19th Century, the most common type of horse in the U.S. was a very versatile animal. After all, it had to be used for the saddle, both for work and for pleasure, and was the product of the crossbreeding of the horses carried to America by the Spanish with different English breeds. This crossbreeding produced a more muscular horse that could cover short distances quickly, commonly

Blackfoot warrior riding an Indian pony. The Red skin warrior's mounts were usually excellent animals with dappled coats, some of which were as sought after as the Appaloosa.

called the 'Quarter Horse' as it could cover a quarter mile at great speed. The horses bred by the settlers and subsequently purchased by the army were driven in small herds to holding areas from where they were assigned to each unit. Their first contact with the riders was usually not exactly a pleasant one: The animals generally cowered, reared up and even bolted. The problem was resolved with the help of troopers who were experts with wild and spirited horses, normally old cowboys who, in exchange for a little extra money, tamed the animals.

That said, unfortunately, riders of this calibre were few and far between and many of the raw recruits were easterners where experience with horses was unusual.

Attempts were made to assign horses of the same colour to the whole of each unit, to facilitate the easy recognition of units at first sight and at a distance. An

A 2nd Cavalry officer's horse in a historical reconstruction. The officers' mounts were, in the main, better bred than those of the troops as they usually sourced and paid for themselves. It is estimated that an army horse would have been able to carry in the region of 240 pounds or more (including the estimated average of 140 pounds for the rider).

example of distribution by battalions and companies could be as follows:

	Bay	Sorrel	Chestnut	Grey
1st Battalion	Co.A	Co.B	Co.C	Co.D
2nd Battalion	Co.E	Co.F	Co.G	Co.H
3rd Battalion	Co.I	Co.K	Co.L	Co.M (*)

In general, the Indian ponies were generally better mounts and, furthermore, each warrior usually owned several horses. Although they were sturdier, resistant to disease and faster over long distances at the long trot, they usually lacked the speed over short or middle distance possessed by some of the army's horses with features similar to those of the Quarter Horse. Hence, it is hardly surprising to read in contemporary records where fortunate officers and troopers on good army mounts saved their scalps due to their horse's speed of acceleration thus escaping their pursuers. The Indian horses were lighter and shorter and fed exclusively on pasture, giving them a greater independence during the months of abundance on the prairies. However, this attribute fell alarmingly during the winter months when available pasture was, more or less, non-existent. The army, on the other hand, depended on a constant supply of forage and if adequate quantities were available, their horses could cover large distances at any time of the year. The long marches demanded a great effort from the horses and the distance covered in the course of a day could vary considerably according to the meteorological conditions and dependency on other slower groups. Custer's 7th Cavalry covered 50 km (31 miles) daily during the Little Bighorn campaign. The same daily mileage was also quoted by General Crook hence it would appear to be quite a common distance on long campaigns. The columns were also able to force march much more when circumstances demanded it. Indeed, Custer managed to attain 105 km (65 miles) daily during his runs in Kansas in 1868 and the 4th Cavalry covered more than 200 km (124 miles) in 32 hours along the Rio Grande, hardly without stopping. Under these conditions, the horses were subjected to exhausting marches that not all of them were able to endure. In extreme circumstances, a number of horses rendered their final service. On top of that, when attacked by hostiles, the cavalryman quite often used horse, dead or alive, saddle and other trappings as a barricade. The horse also served as food when they died.

(*) The horses of various colours that didn't fit into the allocation described were assigned to Company M, which was nicknamed the 'Calico Company'.

Captain Myles Keogh's gelding, Comanche, was the sole surviving horse of the 7th Cavalry at Little Bighorn although, in fact, many more horses survived and were used by the Indians. Its description gives an idea of the typical army horse's features: chestnut, 429 kg (946 pounds) and 15 hands high. It must have been a very resilient horse as it survived serious wounds but was never ridden again and died at the age of 28. Today, it can be found stuffed and on display in the Natural History faculty of the University of Kansas.

HORSE FURNITURE

During the peak of the war against the Indians in 1876, many of the cavalry regiments' horses were still equipped with saddles and other furniture from the Civil War. This equipment was of poor quality given its hasty manufacture and cost cutbacks, essential in order to quickly produce thousands of saddles, bridles and other accessories. The badly cut and died leather gave them an old and tarnished look. While some leather items quickly deteriorated under the harsh climatic conditions of the Great Plains others, such as the bridles and stirrups had to be maintained in good working order.

The U.S. Cavalry regulation saddle was the popular model created by a captain of the 1st Cavalry, George McClellan, in 1855 and it was named after him. The design was based on a Prussian model and remained in use until the First World War with a few modifications. Its wooden frame was very strong and was covered in rawhide. All the saddle pieces were made of black-dyed leather, although it is possible to find models in various hues of brown.

The saddle blanket was placed under the saddle and was made from indigo blue wool. It was

190 cm long (75") by 170 cm wide (67"), but was folded several times until six layers were obtained. It was trimmed with a fringe of 7.62 cm (3"), normally orange and in the centre, appeared the initials 'U.S.'.

The saddle was also used to support the rest of the riding equipment. It was most important to avoid overloading the horse. However, on many occasions, especially when campaigns lasted for months and greater quantities of rations, ammunition and forage had to be carried, as well as extra blankets and ponchos, this was unavoidable. On reconnais-sance or patrol missions or when pursuing the enemy, every unnecessary item was placed in the baggage train. The use of non-regulation articles was also quite common. The officers usually carried different elements including girths made from other materials or a dark blue saddlecloth with a yellow fringe.

Plates A & B

1) 1874 McClellan model saddle
2) Two black leather saddlebags hung from each side of the saddle for storing ammunition, rations, etc.
3) Blanket roll
4) Forage bags carrying horse feed, generally oats.
5) Bag/pouch
6) Nose bag, which was hung from the horse's head for feeding, made of leather and canvas
7) Carbine socket
8) Saddle skirts. They were uncomfortable and the rider often discarded them:
9) Bridles
10) Stirrups. Generally made from walnut or American oak wood, made from a single piece for the troops; the officers' stirrups were made of metal. Some troopers and officers fitted a protective cover at the front.
11) Canteen
12) Tin mug
13) Lariat and picket pin

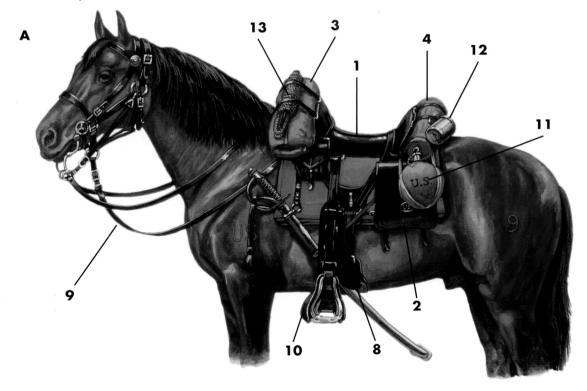

A

B

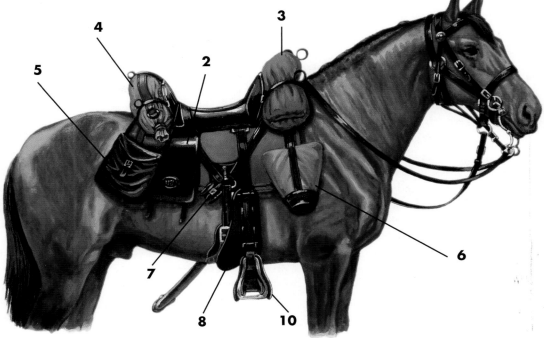

Plate C

1) Binoculars / field glasses and their case.

2) Horse riding gauntlets: They were generally white (White Berlin) or buff.

3) Spurs. They were usually of steel with a simpler design than the officer's gilt/brass ones shown here.

4) 1874 Model canvas and buffalo hide boots, for use in cold temperatures.

5) Riding boots, 1872 Model. They were designed without a distinction between left and right feet. Several models were manufactured with slight variations in design and quality, depending on the supplier.

6) Lariat and picket pin. As trees were rare on the prairies, the only means of picketing a horse was to use an iron stake in the ground.

7) Canteen. Made from metal and covered in canvas or woollen material; some models were stencilled with 'U.S.' on the cover along with the owner's name or other identifying mark.

C

THE EXPLORERS

The Indian Wars were fought over vast territories of thousands of square kilometres, from the west of the Mississippi River to the Rocky Mountains. However, by the middle of the 19th Century, the majority of the Indian people lived on the Central and Northern plains, where the hunting grounds were better. These wide expanses were covered with a never-ending sea of grass and shrubs, crossed by rivers and an abundance of streams that became dry beds and gullies during the dry season. Trees were scarce and the only tree to be found on the prairie was, and is the cottonwood, cousin of the poplars and aspens. The climate was extreme and changeable, erasing and confusing the rare existing landmarks.

The cavalry was responsible for locating and harassing the Indians in these places. When a large tribe was under attack, it divided into smaller groupings until all traces of the large group disappeared in the immense landscape. The most efficient means of finding an Indian was to use another Indian. From 1866, the army was officially authorised to recruit Redskins as scouts, upon whom a crucial part of the mission's success depended.

Indians from the Crow, Ree, Arapahoe, Shoshone, Bannock, Pawnee, Ute, Nez Percé and Osage tribes were most employed used as scouts by the army. It was not easy to persuade an Indian to betray his tribe, thus these scouts usually belonged to an enemy tribe of that being pursued. It was no coincidence that Crow scouts were used in the wars against the Sioux and Cheyenne, their ancestral enemies. Other officers, including the efficient General Crook, managed to successfully persuade Apaches to act as guides in the pursuit of other Apache groups as it was psychologically demoralising to know that they were being betrayed and chased by warriors of their own tribe.

Generals Crook and Terry and the experienced commander of the 4th Cavalry, Ronald Mackenzie, had their favourite Indian scouts whom they trusted implicitly. Custer also had his own Crow scouts leading the 7th Cavalry, showing the way to Little Bighorn including Hairy-Moccasin, Goes-Ahead, White-Man-Runs-Him and Curly. However, the general's favourite scout was Bloody Knife, an Arikara Indian, with whom he became close friends.

Another specie of scouts were the pale faces. These were hunters, trappers, gold prospectors; white men who were familiar with the ways and territory of the Indians. A number even lived among the tribes, having taken an Indian partner and being awarded the sobriquet, 'Squawman' (1). Some knew the terrain as well as the Indians themselves and, being white men, there were no communication problems resulting from culture or mentality, which meant that their opinions were complementary and explained the information provided by the Indian scouts.

Many white scouts rode ahead of the Cavalry. Ton Le Forge, for example, was General Crook's favourite white scout; Savage Hill accompanied General Hancock on his campaign against the Cheyenne; Grouard died with the Seventh at Little Bighorn. By far the most famous was California Joe, Custer's buffoon, who possessed an unpredictable nature and dirty appearance, always rode a mule and wore a large Mexican sombrero. This character represented the stereotypical white scout. His real name was Moses Embrer Milner and he had been a muleteer in the war against Mexico and gold rushes. He got married and fathered two children in Oregon, but his love for the frontier was so great that he abandoned his family and returned to the adventure, his life's real passion. He is always remembered accompanied by his colleague, Jack Corbin.

Occasionally, Indian women were used as scouts. Numerous women were captured during attacks on villages and those who had a deep knowledge of the terrain due to their age and experience were selected. Some, like the Cheyenne 'Me-o-tozi' (she was young and beautiful) became Custer's lover and advisor, with whom it is said that she bore a child.

(1) Squawman: Coming from the word 'squaw' given to Indian women.

Figure 1: California Joe, a white scout used frequently by General Custer. These men tended to wear civilian clothing, often mixed with others of Indian origin. Weaponry varied greatly; on this occasion, he is carrying a Winchester repeating rifle.

Figure 2: Curly, a Crow scout and one of the few survivors from Custer's group at Little Bighorn. A U.S. army officer usually commanded the Redskin scouts. They had no regulation uniform and often mixed their Indian clothing with army-issue items.

Figure 3: A cavalry Lieutenant Colonel. He is wearing the civilian 'fireman'-style shirt, often sported by officers, under a non-regulation 'buckskin' or suede jacket.

THE INDIAN WARS

The Indian Wars lasted for a period of 25 years and consisted of hundreds of isolated battles against a large number of tribes. Within this general term, more specific names stand out such as 'Red Cloud's War', the 'Nez Perce' War' and the 'Pine Ridge Campaign' that encompassed skirmishes, full battles and campaigns all with a common denominator… a single enemy nation, of determined duration and a same underlying cause.

Practically all the Cavalry regiments, from the 1st to the 10th stood out for one reason or another, none more so than the legendary 7th and its popular commander, George Armstrong Custer. However, other, lesser known but experienced Cavalry commanders, such as Colonel Mackenzie of the 4th regiment or General George Crook should not be forgotten. Their Apache, Sioux, Comanche and other adversaries are no less legendary, including Sitting Bull, Crazy Horse, Geronimo, Cochise, and Red Cloud. To outline all these events, characters and battles would be too great a task for this book, but it is worth providing the reader with an explanatory summary.

The Northern Plains

Perhaps the most famous encounters, most well-known Indian nations and most cinematographic placenames are to be found in these lands. The most vitally important settler routes passed through this region: westbound wagon trains, openly encouraged by the government that the army was obliged to protect. However, these were also the most sacred territories of the Cheyenne and the disparate groupings of the Sioux nation led by the likes of Sitting Bull, Crazy Horse and Red Cloud. The Bighorn River valleys and its tributary the Little Bighorn, the Powder and Yellowstone Rivers, the Black Hills, where the reckless Captain Fetterman and his eighty soldiers are buried along with and the many men of the 7th Cavalry.

The most important events began in 1866, along the famous Bozeman Trail, the route that joined the Oregon Trail and linked up with the camps near Virgina City. The famous outposts like Fort Laramie, Fort Reno, Fort Smith and Fort Phil Kearny that gave the army so many headaches, were also located there. Constant pressure from the Sioux and Cheyenne warriors forced the U.S. government, in 1868, to sign a treaty subsequently abandon this route.

Peace, however, was short-lived in this tempestuous region. By 1873, confrontations with the Indians had already been experienced when Northern Pacific Line railroad workers invaded their territory. In 1875, a climax was reached in the region, with the discovery of gold in the sacred Black Hills, resulting in the 1868 Treaty being broken. The consequence of this was the 1876 campaign, culminating in the destruction of the 7th Cavalry. However, the army's constant pressure eventually forced the Sioux Nation and its allies to surrender.

'A Peril of the Plains': An Indian attack on a wagon train. While many of the myriad small battles are largely forgotten, popular memory still tends to remember names such as the Little Bighorn along with others such as the Fetterman Massacre, the Wagon Box Fight and the Rosebud, to name but a few.

The end of the Indian Wars opened up the vast expanses of territory known as the Great Plains, lands that extended from the prairies of Montana to Arizona and New Mexico.

The Indian Wars also ended on the Great Plains. The 1890 Pine Ridge Campaign concluded in a final Sioux revolt. The last vestiges of Indian resistance were extinguished with the massacre at Wounded Knee.

The Central Plains

Comanche, Kiowa, Arapahoe and Cheyenne from the south camped on these plains and were the home to the great herds of thousands of buffalo. Across these lands also passed important railway routes to the west. Significant actions took place, such as General Hancock's fruitless 1867 campaign, the Battle of Beecher Island against the Cheyenne in the summer of 1868 and during the winter of the same year, the winter campaign planned by Sheridan that would end with the massacre of Cheyenne chief Black Kettle's people on the banks of the Washita River by Custer's 7th cavalry. In the 1870s, these territories were subjugated after the Red River War, a group of actions involving more than 3,000 soldiers and in which the 4th, 6th and 8th Cavalries participated and culminating in the confrontations at Palo Duro and the final defeat of the Indians in the Kansas territories.

The North-eastern Territories

Not all the conflicts took place on the Plains, some important, but less-er known ones occurred in the northeastern mountains. The Modoc War of 1872-1873 occurred along the California border that included the ferocious battles of the Lava Beds. The Nez Percé War (1877), against the tribe of the same name led by its charismatic leader Chief Joseph, included the confrontations at White Bird Canyon, Clearwater, and Big Hole in northwestern Oregon. Finally, all these territories were pacified once the wars against the Bannock, Sheepeater and Ute tribes in 1878 and 1879 had been won.

The Southeast

In the arid territories of Arizona and New Mexico, lived some of the most tenacious and hardened enemies of the Cavalry...the Apache. This conflict lasted for 25 years and numerous Cavalry troops took part, including the 4th and the two regiments of black soldiers, the 9th and 10th.

'Indian Battle in Cattle Country', by Frederick Remington.

LITTLE BIGHORN

Little Bighorn is undoubtedly the most famous battle of the Indian Wars. It had its origins with the 1876 campaign following the breaking of the 1868 Treaty by the U.S. government. The objective was to free the territories of the Bighorn River and sacred Black Hills from hostile Indians.

'Massacre', 'disaster' and 'defeat' were words of too great an impact for American society of the time. After all, how could this great nation be defeated by 'savage Indians'? A combination of polemic mistakes and mysteries, a popular and eccentric general and an unexpected and fatal outcome has served to convert this cataclysmic event into a powerful and attractive legend.

Sheridan's Three-arm Hold

General Sheridan was ordered to encircle and destroy the Indian tribes established between the Yellowstone and Rosebud Rivers and the Big Horn mountains. He organised three strong columns emanating from different forts with convergent routes that would block all the possible escape routes from the evasive Redskins. They would be trapped: The Indians could run, but they could not hide.

The most significant column was that of General Crook that left Fort Fettterman, Wyoming, in a northerly direction. It was the strongest contingent, composed of more than 1400 soldiers, amongst which were to be found some companies of the 3rd and 5th Cavalry. General Terry's force was the second group, and included the 7th Cavalry, and left Fort Abraham Lincoln in North Dakota. His mission was to advance westward, following the Yellowstone River, to join up with the third column. This column, under the command of Colonel Gibbon, was a mixture of infantry forces and the 2nd Cavalry units that abandoned Fort Ellis in Montana in an easterly direction. The convergence of the three columns was intended to trap the Indians at some point or another.

The Arm-lock is Broken

Crook's advance was slow, as he wanted to leave no hostiles in his rear. On the 16th of June, he reached the shores of the River Rosebud and, a day later, Crazy Horse's Sioux confronted him. While no tactical victory was ever proclaimed, it was actually a clear strategic tri-

George Armstrong Custer enjoyed great popularity in the U.S. before his final, fatal battle; some historians have speculated about his chances as a candidate for the U.S. presidency for the Democratic Party. In 1876, his rank was Lieutenant Colonel, though he was awarded the provisional rank of General during the Civil War. He had an extravagant and controversial personality, but few doubt his impetuous and fearful character. The Indians nicknamed him 'Son of the Morning Star', a romantic sobriquet for an epic Greek tragedy finale.

umph for the Redskins, forcing Crook to retreat. With that, the overall strategic plan was broken: The strongest column was deactivated and withdrew southwards.

Terry's Doubts

While all this was taking place, further north the other two columns had united at Yellowstone and, on the stern-wheel steamer 'Far West' the pre-battle strategy conference took place and Terry united Custer and Gibbon. The three of them were unaware of General Crook's fate and decided to continue advancing. However, there was one snag, where exactly were the Indians?

Terry ordered for the forward area to be scouted and discovered traces that indicated that the hostiles had headed southwards. He divided his forces: He and Gibbon descended on the right-hand side, climbing up the Yellowstone River and then the Big Horn and entered the Little Bighorn from the north. The other contingent, comprising Custer's 7th Cavalry would make a wider circle to the left, descending along the Rosebud River, and seeking the rear of the Indian group in order to cut off its retreat. It

A) APPROACHING THE BATTLE.

1) Crook's column's approach from the south and his retreat after the defeat at the Battle of Rosebud.

2) Approach of Terry's column.

3) Approach of Gibbon's column.

4) Meeting point between Terry and Gibbon at Yellowstone.

5) Terry and Gibbon's march towards Little Bighorn.

6) March of Custer's 7th Cavalry to Little Bighorn.

B) BATTLE OF LITTLE BIGHORN

1) Great Indian village.

2) Reno's attack on the village from the south.
   2a) Reno's firing line after the failed charge.
   2b) First retreat.
   2c) Second and chaotic retreat crossing the river to the high hill.
   2d) Reno's final resistance, surrounded by Indians in the high hill (actually called Reno's Hill).

3) Benteen's movements.
   3a) Scouting towards the protected south protecting the flank from a village attack.
   3b) Changing course and the advance to join the rest of the regiment.
   3c) Benteen helps to maintain Reno's position.
   3d) Attempt to save Custer led by Wier and Benteen.
   3e) Weir's approach towards Custer (actually called Weir Point).

4) Custer's route in his failed attempt to attack the village from the north.
   4a) Custer's possible routes.
   4b) Yates' group's attempt at attacking the village.
   4c) Possible groups into which Custer's command divided.

5) Attacks by the Indians, led by Crazy Horse, Two Moons and Gall, who surrounded Custer's command.

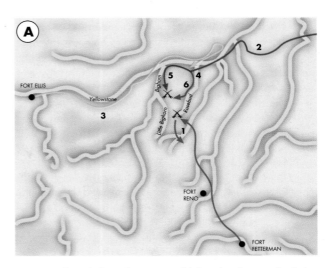

was predicted that Custer would be the first to find the Indians. If that was the case, he was to localise them and await Terry to join him before attacking. Although these were the instructions given to Custer by Terry, he had also given him a margin of manoeuvre in the event of unforeseen circumstances. The doubt over whether Custer disobeyed orders was resolved once and for all.

Bad Forebodings

On the 22nd of June, the 7th departed at speed, covering many miles. Custer was in a hurry and left behind the sabres and musicians: He could no longer afford to carry the tones of GarryOwen (1). If there was to be glory, this conceited commander wanted it all for himself so it was no coincidence that he took with him Mark Kellog, a newspaper reporter who was supposed to cover the success. His men, however, noted suspicious Indian scouts and whispered among themselves…some of them had bad omens: One night, the wind got up and blew over and dragged his personal red and blue guidon. It was rumoured that

(1) A well-known military march that Custer adopted for his regiment, later also popularised by Hollywood.

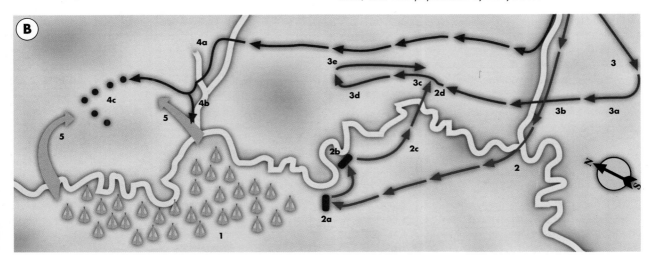

Custer was no longer the resolute commander that he had once been. He had lost his usual good humour. The most superstitious observed the general's silence and noted that he had cut off his long blond pony tail. Even his trusty scout suspected the worse.

At the end of June, temperatures are very high in Montana. Both soldiers and mounts marched, sweating profusely yet and hardly stopping during the 23rd and 24th. They were exhausted. The Indian scouts discovered more and more traces and tension mounted. The clues were clear and unequivocal: A large concentration of hostile Indians was camped in the valley of Little Bighorn. Custer was eager to trap them. Under cover of night, they neared stealthily. Before daybreak, scout Curly saw what appeared to be the smoke from the fires of a great camp. At eight o'clock in the morning on the 25th, the 7th Cavalry approached its fated destiny in the valley.

'Sioux otoe!, Sioux otoe!'

A large concentration of various Sioux tribes such as Cheyenne, Blackfoot and Brulee, were camped on the shores of Little Bighorn. (2) 'Sioux otoe! Sioux otoe!' (many Sioux, everywhere...), Custer's Crow scouts informed him. But Custer was inflexible: At last he had found his prey and if he wiped out the camp, the echoes of his victory would reach as far as Washington. He manoeuvred and attacked the camp from the north and south simultaneously, cutting off any possibility for the Indians to escape. But the impulsive officer committed a number of fateful errors. He failed to reconnoitre the area, had no idea how far the camp extended along the river, the best point for crossing the river and how to realise two coordinated attacks. Another major mistake was that he had left his regiment exposed and had lost the advantage of surprising the enemy. Finally, he disregarded his own experience that had taught him that Indians always stood and resisted an attack while allowing time for their families to escape. Finally, and the biggest mistake of all, the impetuous general sorely underestimated the number of warriors in the encampment. 'We have the 7th with us, Charlie, we are invincible...' he told his scout convinced.

A Fine Day for Dying

After setting out his plans, Custer divided his regiment into two battalions and wished them 'good hunting, sirs...' One of them, under the command of Captain Benteen with H, D and K companies, would scout the hills to the west and whose objective was to cover the flank in case of possible Indian attack. Major Reno, meanwhile, would charge the southern entrance to the camp with A, G and M companies. Custer himself, with C, E, F, I and L companies, would march along the rocky crags to the northeast of the river looking for a place from which to attack the village from the north. The remaining company B, under the command of Captain McDougall, would remain to protect the supply column.

Engraving of Custer's last stand before his death. Many have speculated over the fact that Custer's body was neither mutilated nor scalped. Some find the explanation that he was acknowledged by the Indians and respected for his bravery; others believe that he committed suicide at the last moment and that Indians did not violate the bodies of people who took their own lives.

The plan was put into action. Reno crossed the Little Bighorn River at 15:00 and charged from the south of the village. Meanwhile, Custer started his gallop in search of a place to attack from the north. From the heights he had a complete view over the Indian encampment, will have realised its size and must have seen Reno charge. Did he doubt his victory at that moment? We will never know, but he sent two very significant messages. With the first, he ordered B Company, which had stayed behind with the supply column, to come forward. Somewhat later, he gave the famous order to Benteen: 'Come on... big village, be quick... bring packs' It was 15:45 and very hot on the prairies of Montana.

The Tragedy Unfolds

Reno, fearing a trap, halted his charge on the Indian village. He dismounted his men and set up a firing line against the enormous number of Indians that surged forward both from ahead and against his left flank. The faint-hearted officer lost control and fell prey to panic. Some say that he was delirious. The defence line degenerated into total confusion and retreated towards the thicket and small wood at the edge of the river. In this dramatic retreat, Reno's men saw no alternative but to cross the river in disorganised groups and, with a varying degrees of luck, they fled in terror to the protection of the rocky crags.

Benteen, responding to Custer's order, dug in his heels to follow the General's tracks, but met with the demoralised Reno. While his timely arrival saved Reno from possible annihilation, he did not then continue in aid of his General, as he had been ordered to.

Meanwhile, Custer divided his forces yet again, this time into two groups (3), one to the left under the command of Captain Yates (companies E and F) that would try to cross the river, attack the village and alleviate the pressure on Reno while the other (companies C, I and L) would await reinforcements on the hill, later named Calhoun Hill. Finally, the first group's attempt to cross the river failed and the two groups were overcome by the great concentration of Indians that had surrounded them and blocked their northern and eastern exits.

Custer's men were, by now, being cut down. Captain Wier, commanding D company (in the hills with Reno), set off downstream in an attempt to locate Custer, later being followed by Benteen and companies H, K and M. They made some progress to the north and looked for signs of Custer and his command, but they only found smoke and confusion in the distance and were soon harassed by numerous Indians. They then retreated to Reno's hill and the group that managed to hold out until the arrival of Terry's troops.

The final moments of Custer's command must have been dramatic: The soldiers were bunched together in various groups and they improvised their defence. Some fell prey to panic, spread out and were hunted like rabbits. Others surrendered and were killed or committed suicide. The most valiant sold their lives dearly. Finally, the killing ground descended into silence as the last man slumped dead. Was it Custer himself, no one will ever know! Almost all were scalped and savagely mutilated. Custer's corpse was found on the hill that today bears his name, naked with a bullet hole in the temple and another in the chest. While his ears had been pierced, he was not mutilated and his hair was intact. By his side, 17 Remington rifle cartridges were found.

(2) Over the years, the number of warriors who fought at Little Bighorn has been greatly debated. The most approximate totals corresponding to most reliable research vary between 1500 and 3000 effectives.

(3) Other researchers are not convinced that Custer undertook this manoeuvre.

The Little Bighorn battlefield today, featuring a number of the gravestones of the 7ᵗʰ Cavalry. Archaeological excavations have provided explanations for what happened to Custer and his men, although any theorizing is always surrounded by contradictory data. Many survivors swore not to provide any more information about the events while Custer's widow remained alive, but she outlived them all.

CUSTER'S TROOPS

The 7th Cavalry was a veteran unit in the Indian Wars as, since 1866, it had participated in numerous combat actions against the Redskins. Its commander, General George A. Custer, could also count on his earlier experiences fighting against Indians and had reliable scouts as advisors. However, his regiment's lack of officers had a direct affect on his fateful ending. Of the 44 officers theoretically assigned, 13 did not take part in the campaign and of the 718 NCO's and enlisted troops, 152 never even left Fort Lincoln. This situation was made worse by the fact that approximately 20 % of his troopers were, more or less, raw recruits who had neither the experience or skill required for the battle.

Custer was a demanding taskmaster, as was habitual with him, and he had embarked on exhausting forced marches during the days preceding the battle. This had undoubtedly diminished his command's combat ability. A number of his subordinates, among whom featured Major Reno and Captain Benteen who both played an important role in the turn of events, did not form part of the group of Custer's loyal followers, led by his brother Thomas Custer, captain of C company, and had openly expressed clear disagreement with their superior. This disaffection may have affected the affair.

Little Bighorn represented the culmination of a typical campaign to seek and destroy Indian villages. It is estimated that the Indians were capable of breaking camp in twenty minutes and, once on the march, could cover 80 Km (50 miles) daily. In contrast, a normal army column, slowed by its supply train, usually covered an average of 50 km (31 miles) a day. This led experienced commanders during the Indian Wars to become obsessed with preventing camped Indians from escaping once they had been located.

Custer, aware of the Indian's mobility, left behind all but essential equipment and carried provisions for just 15 days. He refused to carry along the famous Gatling machine guns offered him by General Terry, rightly arguing that they were too heavy. However, as events turned out, it was much less wise to refuse to include a number of companies from the 2nd Cavalry, reinforcements that, perhaps, might have saved him from annihilation. As always, Custer wanted all the responsibility and glory for his own regiment.

The 7th Cavalry's total losses at the Battle of Little Bighorn were 286 dead (197 with Custer) and 55 wounded, including the 16 officers, scouts and some civilians accompanying them.

Yellowstone River, 22nd June, 1876. The 7th Cavalry's departure date for the valley of Little Bighorn.

During the hot summers, the jacket was tightly rolled up at the back of the saddle and the majority of the men rode in shirtsleeves. These shirts were of a wide variety of models and sources, and it was quite normal for soldiers to use their oldest ones on campaign, keeping the better quality ones for ceremonial occasions. The constant high temperatures were so debilitating for the soldiers that, in 1871, the State of Texas officially authorised the use of white trousers and straw hats was for all officers and men. This ruling that was later extended to all the territories south of Washington DC.

Figure 1: Corporal of the 7th Cavalry. In 1872, a new work jacket was introduced, with bright yellow on the cuffs, collar and chest, pleated and fastened with nine buttons. This model was not very popular and was rapidly replaced. He wears the 1872 Model army issue trousers, with two pockets opening at the top and a yellow stripe corresponding to the rank of corporal. On his head is a non-regulation straw hat worn by many soldiers at Little Bighorn. These could be purchased from the Far West steamboat (climbing up the Yellowstone in the background). As in Fig. 2, he is armed with an 1873 Model Springfield carbine and an 1873 Single-Action Army Colt revolver.

Figure 2: Private, 7th Cavalry. He wears a grey flannel army issue shirt with two pockets and buttoned to the middle of the chest, commonly used until 1881. He has an 1872-pattern folding hat, with wide flaps and fasteners on each side so they could be raised and fixed at the top. It was the most unpopular campaign hat because it lacked consistency, quickly deteriorated and equally quickly lost its shape.

Figure 3: Lieutenant Colonel George Armstrong Custer (he was termed 'General' as this was the provisional rank he held during the Civil War). He wears a 'fireman-style' non-regulation shirt, very popular among the officers, and regimental number embroidered on the collar. He also sports a red neckerchief, Custer's favourite colour for this style of uniform. A senior officers' mode of dress was very personal and usually did not conform to the regulation dress. On his ill-fated, final campaign, he wore buckskin trousers with scout-style fringing and a wide-brimmed white or light cream coloured slouch hat, both items of civilian origin. His side arms were also peculiar to him and included two English revolvers: a double-action .44 calibre Webley Galand and a Somerville, also called 'The Bulldog'.

A hunting knife, decorated with Indian motifs, is also visible hanging from the waist.

47

THE APACHE WARS

Apaches! simply mentioning the name invoked fear in the most veteran cavalryman. The so-called 'Apache Wars' lasted throughout the 1870s with ongoing campaigns against their leader, Cochise, and during 1870s and 1880s against Victorio and Geronimo. The conflict developed in the southern states and also included those bordering Mexico: Texas, New Mexico and Arizona. This last state especially remains today quintessential in the legend of the Wild West created by Hollywood as the land of Apaches, silver, gold and copper mines, cowboys, the Earps and Clantons and their legendary fight at Tombstone's OK Corral. This territory was known as 'The Land of Standing-Up Rocks', after its magnificent canyons and other geological formations that, seemingly, defied the laws of gravity.

The Troublesome Southern Indians

The Apache had already been implacable enemies of the Mexican Army and, with the arrival of the new settlers and the development of economic interests in the region; they fought with the same tenacity as their northern neighbours. As in the Great Plains, the Government put into practice its policy of displacing the Indians from their traditional hunting grounds onto reservations and establishing a chain of forts to control the defined territory.

The first conflict took place in the 1870s against the western Apache Indians, also called Navajos, who were confined on the Fort Summer Reservation following their final surrender at Canyon de Chelly. However, other Apache tribes did not submit easily and resisted tenaciously led by very able chiefs such as Mangas Coloradas, Cochise and Victorio. The U.S.

Government called on General George Crook to subjugate these obstinate savages. He led a series of campaigns over a period of two decades against stubborn resistance until Cochise finally signed a peace treaty. The Indian chief accepted the confinement of his people on four reservations in New Mexico and Arizona.

However, that was not the end of the matter. Crook's success was not total and groups of Indians led by Victorio and a new leader, Geronimo, never accepted that the final fate of the Apache people was to be confined on reservations. Victorio died in 1881, but Geronimo and a small band of faithful warriors continued their resistance. His tenacious struggle became legendary, marked by a savage guerrilla war and always dismissive of Crook's attempts to reach an agreement. Geronimo and his Apaches forged a legend of fear and hate unleashed by a spiral of violence and desire for vengeance that was nurtured by the suspicion of the lack of respect for agreements between Crook and the Indian leader.

Finally, the government, after visiting the failed diplomat Crook, replaced him with Nelson Miles. He immediately raised a force of no less than 5,000 soldiers reinforced with 500 Apache scouts, to seek out and capture a group of Indians consisting of just 36 warriors and 80 women and children! Geronimo and his group held out for five months before finally being trapped at Skeleton Canyon by Lieutenant Gatewood and his Chiricahua guides. He finally surrendered and was sent to the reservation.

The Apache Warrior

Few tribes of the Great Plains were as skilled in warfare as the Apache. Ambushes, incursions and kidnaps were their specialisation. Their method of conducting and understanding war was encapsulated in a sole word: 'Nagondzog'.

The Apache warrior was an expert at survival. His strategy was based on a profound knowledge of each trail, well, canyon, gorge and gully through which he passed. Their low numbers were compensated for through the use of deceit, trickery and shrewdness instead of boasting and bravery of the Plains Indians that caused them many casualties. Because of their deviousness, the soldiers often accused them of cowardice and treachery. However, when cornered, they unleashed their true tenaciousness and terrible ferocity on the adversary.

The Apaches raids were an integral part of their economy and were the means of gaining a supply of horses, food and possessions. They were probably the finest riders and shots ever confronted by the U.S. Cavalry. They rode their horses to death, ate them to survive and took another horse. They moved in small groups of between five to twelve warriors travelling through the mountains by day and the valleys by night. They scoured the dusty places in the hills in search of enemies

U.S. Army Officers photographed at an Apache camp in Arizona in 1875.

General George Crook (on the right) in talks with Geronimo.

and, if necessary, hid for four days without sleep and hardly eating. They kept their personal possessions to the minimum and were capable of covering 120 km (75 miles) a day across the inhospitable Arizona desert.

Crook's Tactics

George Crook quickly became aware of the overwhelming deficiencies of his troops. They lacked both the experience and the territorial knowledge and, furthermore, they didn't have the determination and innate resistance of the Apache. To defeat such an obdurate enemy, he saw the necessity of hiring as many other Apaches as was necessary: *'To catch an Apache, you have to use another one'*. He was also surrounded himself with experienced, efficient officers such as Colonel Benjamin Grierson and loyal units like the 9th and 10th Cavalries. In short, he utilised units renowned for their tenacious persecution and strategy. To achieve his aims, he freed his columns from the slow supply trains and replaced them with faster haulage mules thus increasing their movement capacity by 34 km (21 miles) a day. However, even with all of Crook's efficiency, only an immense outnumbering could break Geronimo.

Geronimo or Goyathlay (one who yawns) was both the spiritual and war leader of the Apache. In 1876, the army received the order to confine the Chiricahua on the San Carlos Reservation. Geronimo affected his escape and took refuge in Mexico, crossing the frontier time and time again, always successfully eluding the U.S. and Mexican troops. For almost a decade, the sensationalist press profited from exaggerating Geronimo's activities, creating a false legend of an assassin and traitor.

BUFFALO SOLDIERS

The legend of the US Cavalry fades once again with mention of the 9th and 10th regiments, both of which were formed from Afro-American recruits. During the Civil War, 178,000 black men served in the Union Army and, in recognition of their service, in 1866, Congress authorised the creation of six regiments of coloured men, two of which were to be cavalry regiments. Two recruitment centres were established specifically for these units in New Orleans, Louisiana, and Louisville, Kentucky. It was the Cheyenne and Comanche Indians who awarded them the epithet 'Buffalo-Soldiers', which appears to have originated from their curly dark hair and reddish skins that reminded them of the buffalo's coat. For some strange reason, the Indians did not like fighting these soldiers, though they soon came to appreciate their bravery and tenacity in battle. *'Buffalo soldier no good, bad medicine'*, they used to say. Neither is it known why the Indians never scalped them. The soldiers of the 9th and 10th, were not offended by the nickname and carried it with pride. The name remains in use even to this day.

While these two regiments were composed and armed the same as the rest of the Cavalry regiments, the officers were white. The NCOs and troopers were subjected to constant racial discrimination, not just from their comrades in arms in other cavalry regiments but also from their own officers, many of whom considered an assignment to these regiments as an insult. Moreover, the treatment meted out to them by the white settlers they were assigned to protect was even more unpleasant. Paradoxically, their efficiency was praised when fighting side-by-side with other, white units and instances of desertion in these regiments were extremely low. Some feature writers of the era quickly recognised that their discipline, tenacity, fighting spirit and suffering was above the average demonstrated by other units composed of white men. Evidence of this is the fact that Congress awarded a total of 22 Medals of Honour to these units.

Until 1890, they participated in numerous and important actions against the Indians in Kansas and the Dakotas. However, it was in the southern territories such as New Mexico, Arizona and Texas were their participation was best felt.

Santa Cruz Valley (Arizona) 1885. 10th Cavalry. Campaign against Geronimo.

In the spring of 1885, the 10th Cavalry redeployed to Texas in the Arizona territory to take part in the campaign unleashed against Geronimo and his Chiricahua Apache band. Eleven companies were moved from Fort Davis, to which company 'I' was joined at Camp Rice, and for the first time in history, the whole of the 10th, including its musical band, marched together.

Figure 1: Sergeant of the 10th Cavalry. He wears an 1883 fatigue blouse. The unpopular item of clothing from 1872, pleated and with nine buttons, was quickly replaced by another with five buttons and a simpler design. The initial models, such as that from 1874 that still bore the yellow on the cuffs and collar, disappeared in 1883 and were replaced by a simple model worn by this sergeant fighting against the Apache. This NCO wears buckskin boots of Indian origin, more comfortable for the hot territories of Arizona and New Mexico. He is wearing a civilian straw hat and carries a non-regulation blanket across the saddlebow. Like his comrades, he is armed with an 1873 Model Springfield carbine and an 1873 Model Single-Action Army Colt revolver.

Figure 2: Private of the 10th Cavalry. He is equipped with a bright blue 1882 shirt with yellow edging replacing the earlier more sober grey shirts. The 1882 hat was fitted with ventilation holes. He is wearing a civilian colourful neckerchief and a 'Mills'-type belt, made of blue cloth piped yellow. The buckle is an H-shaped brass one, inscribed with 'U.S.' that began to be issued during this period.

Figure 3: Apache scout. During the wars against the Apache, many scouts from the same tribe accompanied the cavalry. There was no general ruling on scout uniforms until 1890 hence this scout wears the usual clothing of his tribe, including the typical ribbon tying up his long hair. Instead of a carbine, he carries an infantry-model Springfield rifle that, although longer than the carbines, had a greater range and accuracy.